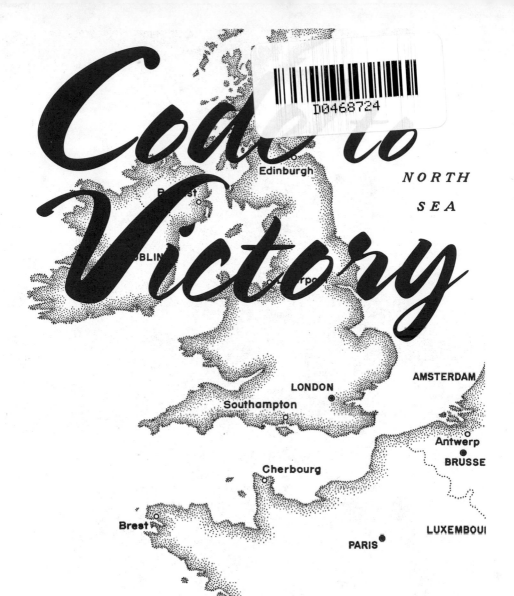

Code to Victory

D0468724

NORTH SEA

Edinburgh

Belfast

DUBLIN

Liverpool

LONDON

Southampton

AMSTERDAM

Antwerp

BRUSSE

Cherbourg

Brest

PARIS

LUXEMBOUI

Coming of Age
in World War II

Code to Victory

—◦—

Coming of Age
in World War II

by
Arnold C. Franco
as told to
Paula Aselin Spellman

Sunflower University Press®
1531 Yuma • P. O. Box 1009 • Manhattan, Kansas 66505-1009 USA

To fellow Rotarian Berk, Paula Spellman 1999

Poetry credits:

Browning: The Poetical Works of Robert Browning (Boston, MA: Houghton Mifflin Company, 1974).

Finneran, Richard J., ed. *The Poems of W. B. Yeats: A New Edition* (New York: Macmillan Publishing Co., 1983). Reprinted with permission of Simon & Schuster. Copyright © 1983 by Anne Yeats.

Johnston, John H. *English Poetry from the First World War* (Princeton, NJ: Princeton University Press, 1964).

Rudyard Kipling: Selected Verse (New York: Penguin Books, Ltd., 1977).

Layout by Lori L. Daniel

ISBN 0-89745-232-1

Sunflower University Press is a wholly-owned subsidiary of the non-profit 501(c)3 Journal of the West, Inc.

As I approach my 50th wedding anniversary, I dedicate **Code to Victory** *to my family — to my wife Beverly for her support of all my endeavors throughout our marriage, and to our four children, Debra, Wendy, Miriam, and Edmond.*

The Franco crest — *Under peace plenty.*

In 1492, 15th-century Spain, my forefathers had been amongst the first victims of the Inquisition, the radical purging of the Jews.

In 1942, mid-20th century, we faced the Second Grand Inquisitor, Adolf Hitler.

When You Are Old

When you are old and grey and full of sleep,
And nodding by the fire, take down this book,
And slowly read, and dream of the soft look
Your eyes had once, and of their shadows deep. . . .
                                        W. B. Yeats

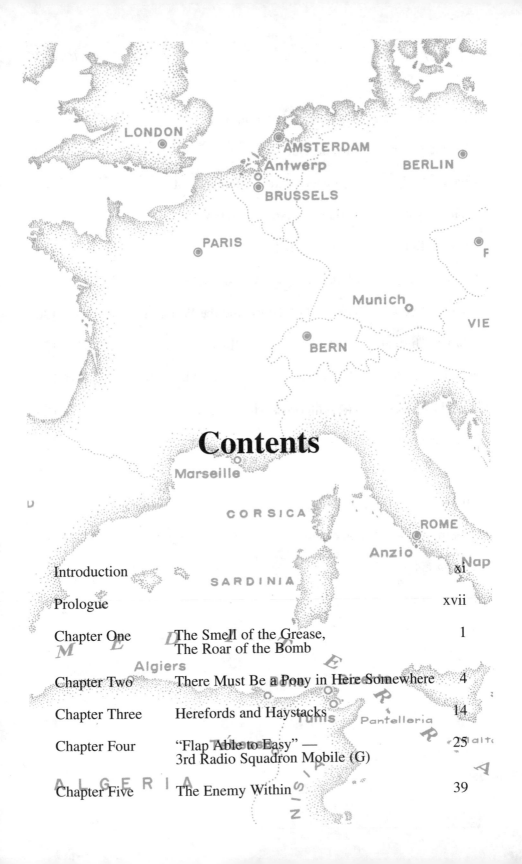

Contents

Introduction

MY DISCHARGE PAPER of December 2, 1945, reads:

Cryptanalyst: Broke down German code; work was of a highly secret nature; operational methods and procedures cannot be divulged; intercepted German voice radio messages. . . .

———————◆———————

It is a daunting task to write a personal story more than 50 years after the events — as well as the history of one's outfit — when the two are inextricably mixed. Another veteran, William B. Folkestead, clearly expressed the difficulty in *The View from the Turret*:

> The research, the interviews, the entire preparation of this manuscript can only be likened to plunging into the passage cut by a now distant vessel. Leaping into the waters every effort is expended to catch up before the wake closes, erasing forever any trace of passage.

In the years since the war, I have reflected upon my experiences, and have come to understand that war is not only about violence, but about the explication and resolution of a giant drama on a stage called the battleground, which the military so aptly calls "the theater." Layer upon layer of scenes unfold — stories that fit together as strategies were planned, maneuvers executed, and alliances formed. Lives are changed because of brilliance, stupidity, absurdity, and luck.

The men who grew up in the theater of World War II were left with a pride as no war has done since. They knew what they were fighting for, who the enemy was, and what the price might be. Youth itself presented a facade of naiveté that offered protection from the reality of death. But these men willingly offered their lives to protect their country, and in so doing, gained a respect for each individual's part in achieving that goal. They brought home indelible memories that would influence the remainder of their lives, and many were to find that nothing again would bring the passion and fearful excitement as the war years had. Everything they have done since has been measured through the eyes of World War II and reflected in the words of General George S. Patton: "Compared to war, all other forms of human endeavor shrink to insignificance."

The function of my unit, 3rd Radio Squadron Mobile (G) — for German — in Europe had been to act as a roving ear, listening to both the wireless — Morse Code — and oral German radio transmissions connected primarily with the activities of the German Air Force. This select group, hand-picked by its creator and commanding officer, received the Presidential Unit Citation, but didn't fully realize the impact of their work until 50 years later when the U.S. government declassified the documents telling the story of "Y" — Wireless — Intelligence. A report prepared by Diane T. Putney of the Office of Air Force History, for the Society for Military History, on April 19, 1996, states:

> Y intelligence has to this day remained hidden in the shadow
> of ULTRA high-grade signals intelligence [*and*] authors have
> neglected Y intelligence . . . because the records supporting its
> history are difficult to locate and many are only recently being
> declassified and released to the public.

In 1994, as a result of the D-Day anniversary celebration, I began to
pursue more seriously a possible meeting of 3rd RSM members. Each
time I contacted one of the men, we journeyed back into memories. Some
felt gratitude, others guilt — guilt for the gift of these extra years, given at
random. Some talked about the end of the war, but for others the end had
never come; the memories were too deep, imprinted as a birthmark upon
the soul. Each of these men had been chosen. Each had faced the enemy
with the exuberance and ignorance of youth. Some had grown old and
weary, others had become vibrant.

The problems I encountered, as a "would be" historian, in order to tell
this story, were compounded by various factors. First, many of the recollections of the men did not match the unit histories and other official documents. And because experience has shown neither source to be infallible,
it was decided to include both versions, where possible, and let the reader
form a conclusion.

Another challenge related to the limited contact the GIs had with each
other during the war, both as individuals and as a group. During the European campaign, the squadron's detachments operated independently from
one another, preventing outside friendships from developing. And at the
end of the war, 3rd RSM was together only a short time before being transported home. We subsequently never had a reunion, and any contacts
between the men were initiated only on an individual basis. This made
finding squadron members a painstaking one-by-one affair, relying on
word-of-mouth to locate each interviewee. In addition, for over 50 years
the veterans had honored the *pledge of secrecy* imposed during our training, and some still found it difficult to share information.

Perhaps the greatest difficulty was in obtaining official records from
military and archival sources because some documents had been destroyed
in a St. Louis warehouse fire over 30 years ago, and others were still
secret. After more than a year, only four pages of one of our operations
reports, from October 1944, had been gathered, and it was *censored*. It was
not until the late 1980s that most of these documents were declassified by

the National Security Agency, and August of 1996 when the critique of the Battle of the Bulge ULTRA intercept information — the British code for the complex German intercepts — was finally released.

Struggling to obtain anything that would assist my quest, the journey turned into an adventure, and often I experienced a sense of amazement at an unexpected meeting of a person, or the finding of a letter, diary, or old photo. The most important break occurred in September 1996. On a tip, I called Bolling Air Force Base in Washington, D.C., and found myself speaking to Diane Putney.

When I identified myself and my mission, there was a slight gasp at the other end of the line.

"You know," she said, "I never thought I'd meet anyone from your squadron." She had recently presented her report to the Society for Military History on the effectiveness of Signal Intelligence in World War II, and our unit's achievements had been amongst the highlights.

During the next year, Putney supplied a wealth of materials (including my squadron's unit histories), which she had used in her research, and directed me to additional information. I owe her a debt of gratitude for her personal attention and effort on my behalf.

I am also greatly indebted to the late Julius Belinkoff — doctor, scientist, and humanist — who not only was one of the first to encourage me to write this book, but helped me get off the "starting block."

To the veterans of the 3rd Radio Squadron Mobile, 9th Air Force, who sent their recollections and memorabilia, and most of all shared the desire to have our story told, a mere thanks is inadequate. This book could not have been as rich without their help:

From 3rd RSM, 9th Air Force:
William C. Brinson, Jr.	John F. O'Hara
Andrew J. Copp III	Henry Schueftan
Hugh M. Davidson	William W. Shaughnessy
Ferdinand Gottlieb	Robert Siefert
Albert J. Gruber	Hyman T. Silverstein
Buford Henry	Kurt S. Tannenwald
James A. McNab	F. L. P. (Peter) White

From others in the 9th Air Force:
Colonel Edward Hitchcock	Colonel Jerry S. Stover
Colonel William Reed	Colonel Harold Stuart

To the families of the late Major (at that time Lieutenant) Mortimer R. Proctor, Jr., Operations Officer of Detachment A, and Colonel Harry R. Turkel, Commanding Officer of our squadron, special appreciation is in order. The diaries and letters from 1944-1945 that they so graciously shared helped to create the framework of the book.

After I had begun this research and writing process, Roger Franco, my cousin, helped me in the construct of my memoirs. As an autodidact — a bard who is fluent in the works of Yeats and Homer — some of his Homeric epithets appeared in the original memoir and have been incorporated into this book. I owe much to his participation.

Throughout the project I was enthusiastically supported by Frank Carnaggio, former editor of *The Ninth Flyer*, the official newsletter of the 9th Air Force Association, Inc. Carnaggio's on-going encouragement assisted me in not succumbing to the doubts of producing yet "another military memoir" — a doubt I hope others will ignore when they consider writing theirs.

Another thank you goes to Terry Mitchel for putting all other work aside to edit *Code to Victory*. Without her effort and excellent work, the manuscript would have been significantly delayed.

I was also assisted from abroad by a number of individuals. Douglas Roberts of Edinburgh — ex-intercept operator for the 382nd Wireless Unit, Royal Air Force, 1943-1945 — supplied the details regarding his part in the training of the initial cadre of Detachment B. In addition, three European women were instrumental in providing material: Mademoiselle Laurence Croise of Paris helped with research and the planning of my trips to Normandy and the Ardennes; Madame Rodolphe Sagehomme of Jalhay, Belgium, constructed an intricate map showing the exact location of von der Heydte's command post during the Battle of the Bulge; and Madame Fiorella Ernst, granddaughter of the countess whose castle billeted Detachment D near the end of the war, provided additional information when we met serendipitously during my trip to Belgium in 1997.

Once the interviews had been completed and transcribed, and the government documents gathered, I looked at a file drawer full of paper and realized that I had a daunting task before me. Several months passed and a story arrived from Paula Spellman, a writer from California, about the *Queen Elizabeth II* crossing to France for the 50th anniversary of D-Day. Later, as the idea for *Code to Victory* developed, I realized how much I had enjoyed and appreciated her writing and felt that she was the appropriate one to help tell my story.

Considering that it is now more that 50 years since the men of 3rd RSM took the *pledge of secrecy* and the government has declassified the documents pertaining to our work, I feel comfortable disclosing in *Code to Victory* what I know and have learned about this unusual outfit.

It is my hope that *Code to Victory* will help preserve the wake that was cut by the 3rd Radio Squadron Mobile (G), 9th Air Force, from Normandy to Weimar, and the multitude of places between during those eventful days from June 9, 1944, to May 8, 1945, V-E Day — *Victory in Europe* — when the German surrender was announced.

ACF

Prologue

I WAS NO DIFFERENT *from the others. Cut from the same olive-drab cloth, impregnated with chemicals, arms folded, shoulders squared. Stacked in readiness, we waited as a long line of young faces inched forward.*

I was handed over to my new owner. He was 19 . . . from New York, filled with the patriotic bravado of youth. Reality would soon rub it off.

As we toiled together throughout the war, shoulder to shoulder, an unspoken bond formed. Soon the smell of his sweat would overcome my foul chemical odor.

When he was a young man, my value went unrecognized. He was proud to be seen with me, but it wasn't until our later years that our roles clarified. In some ways I protected him. People looked at me first, with gratitude; it was only then that they looked at him. Later, I would identify him, telling the world who he was, and what he had done. With me he gained entrée. With me he learned humility. Often his tears wet me more than his sweat.

In later years he would come to me, look me over, contemplate his memories, and occasionally decide to take me along. His fingers would caress my fabric, looking for signs of age. Perhaps I was a reflection of his own advancing years; and if I passed muster, so might he.

Lately, we have been spending more time together — journeys to France, England, and Belgium where I had come into my own. My medals — his — dangled from a rainbow of ribbons pinned to my chest. No one asked what they were for, but they knew where we had been. At random, in the midst of that long-ago conflict, he had been given extra years. We've been together now for over 50.

Today, in his reverie, he came to me again, removed me from the mothballs, and shook the creases from my chest. His arms slipped through my sleeves, he pulled at my brass buttons, and together we faced the mirror.

————◄○►————

> *Compared to war, all other forms of human endeavor shrink to insignificance.*
> — General George S. Patton

Chapter One

The Smell of the Grease, The Roar of the Bomb

T HE LONG NIGHT was cold and tense. The men of Detachment B on duty in Jalhay, Belgium, were huddled in a tent where decks of Poker and Pinochle were dealt to occupy hands and minds. Pay call had been the previous day and they were itching to test their skill and luck. Others sat around on camp stools or cots drinking beer or writing letters home. Friendly bantering bounced back and forth as someone asked for a copy of the *Stars and Stripes*, the Army newspaper, and another quipped, "Shit, can you read?" An occasional curse drifted from the Poker players as their losses mounted. But it was mostly a smoky, peaceful scene that was enveloped by the dark lonely countryside.

Earlier the roar of a German V-1 "buzz" bomb had stopped the game. The air had suddenly become silent and no one uttered a sound. The tent's canvas walls whipped in and out and the bottles on the table rattled precariously. Then stillness engulfed the men. A roar, a moment of silence, an explosion, and it was over. The air seemed to sigh, and the card games continued. The men had begun to relax again, when the calm once more exploded. The unmistakable sounds of diving planes and the staccato firing of machine guns invaded the night. Although the bursts were close, the men dashed through the tent flap to peer into the blackened sky, trying to catch sight of the invisible planes. Dazzling streaks of red tracers darted wildly and then suddenly died away, leaving an unsettled eerie quiet. The men straggled back into the tent and those who had won returned to the Poker table to count their gain. Empty smudged beer bottles sat on the tables, newspapers littered the cots, and flecks of cinder from the small stove blackened the floor, ground in by combat boots. It was a messy, inhospitable place to receive visitors. But then none were expected.

The men began to quiet down and drift off into their individual reverie. Attention was focused elsewhere, when the tent flap opened. A bedraggled British soldier, covered with gasoline and streaked with grime, stood there staring at the amazed men. It seemed a long time before he spoke. "Mind if I come in? I'd like to see the officer in charge."

"What happened?" someone asked, as another grabbed the phone.

"Got mixed up in a bad show." He wearily sat down on an empty chair and stared with vacant eyes. "What didn't happen would be better," he almost whispered as he hung his head.

By then Lieutenant Peter White, Detachment B's Operations Officer, was on the line.

"There's an RAF Sergeant down here, Lieutenant, who'd like to speak to you. Looks like he's in trouble."

It took some time for White to get across the icy ground from his quarters in the hotel to the men's tent. When he arrived, he faced the Brit, whose shoulders hung limp. Sitting before Lieutenant White, his eyes held the ground as he tried to gain some sense of where he was and what had happened. "I couldn't help it, Sir. I did everything I could, but he just kept slipping. He just slipped and slipped and I couldn't stop him."

The British soldier's bomber group had left England early that evening for Germany. When his plane reached its target, it dropped its load and was immediately hit by flak. The navigator was killed outright. The soldier, the skipper of the crew, ordered his men to bail out, but the tail gunner yelled that he had no chute.

"It's okay," the skipper told him. "Jump with me. Just hold on tight and you'll be fine."

"But it wasn't fine, Sir. He started shouting at me. I couldn't hear him, but I knew. I could feel his hands slide from my waist. He was holding on as tight as he could, but the wind was too strong. I could feel his fingers digging into my legs. Finally he was clutching my feet; then he was ripped off by the force of the wind. It seemed to take forever to watch him hit the ground. I tried not to look, but I had to. He was my buddy. He bounced, Sir . . . he bounced."

Everyone seemed to get "Expert" marks. It didn't do much good for a soldier's morale to send him into combat thinking he couldn't hit the enemy.

Chapter Two

There Must Be a Pony in Here Somewhere

HUDDLED ON THE TARMAC shivering in the cold spring of the Washington afternoon, I did my best to protect him, but I was not yet made of the thick woolen cloth that would come with later uniforms. As the slant of the sun became more acute, I sensed that there would be no warmth for him this day, for the frosty wind sweeping across the runway was nothing to the chill of fear that penetrated his marrow. I watched the little group — the chosen ten — linger uncertainly. They knew they had been picked for special duty, but did not yet know what it was. They knew that they had been singled out, but they didn't know why. They knew that their comrades were being transported by ship, not plane. They were unsure. There were so many questions.

Why were they being sent to England on a plane filled with VIPs? Why hadn't they been briefed? Why were they flying instead of sailing? What was the hurry?

With a nonchalance no one felt, they each ground their final cigarette into the asphalt.

Standing at attention with his buddies in the frigid cold, I sensed he felt contradiction. These ten men were unique, but the brass — the Colonels and Generals — brushed past without acknowledgment and stepped to the front of the plane. In turn, his group was sent to the rear. He thought about his training camp in Georgia — with the segregation of the blacks. Now he felt the extent of segregation of the military.

———————◄o►———————

The ten of us arrived on the tarmac through a long and laborious training. It was March 1943. Months earlier than expected, I had found myself reporting for Infantry training at Camp Wheeler in Macon, Georgia, where military life confronted me. What had seemed like an adventure while sitting in my living room in Queens, New York, came quickly into focus with a gun in my hand.

If I had ever entertained the idea of glory in the infantry, the simulated combat assignments forced me to face reality. How "simulated" is it with live ammo flying 2½ feet above your head? Keeping my damn head and butt down was the whole game. Intelligence mattered naught. In training, on my belly, I had crawled low — very low — across slimy fields of thick mud feeling its cold wetness ooze its way through my clothes and pierce my skin with its chill. I was declared "dead" a number of times by the superiors judging my ability to survive.

The 25-mile marches with full packs and maneuvers in pitch-black nights strengthened my body and instilled confidence, but when I returned to my barracks and lay in my bunk staring at the beam above, reality became the monster that could not be kept at bay. I even questioned the value of my expert marksmanship awards for all the weapons I had been trained to use — carbine, M-1, light machine gun, Browning Automatic Rifle — and later found that I was wise to doubt. Everyone seemed to get "Expert" marks. It didn't do much good for a soldier's morale to send him into combat thinking he couldn't hit the enemy. As I grunted and sweated through the exercises, my glasses became a problem, and the term "fog of war" had a distinct personal meaning. I couldn't see with them on or off. Every time I put them on, my body heat made them fog up. I felt exposed and vulnerable. I faced the probability that I wouldn't survive the war if I went overseas as an infantryman.

After I had been at Camp Wheeler for several months, my superiors had noticed my bayonet skills learned while on the high school fencing team, and because my records showed my fluency in Spanish, I was pulled out of my unit to become the bayonet instructor for a battalion of Puerto Rican recruits. Being a "superior" was a role I liked much better, but it didn't do much to assuage my disappointment as I watched my buddies ship off to exotic-sounding Tunisia. At the time, it was hard finding the pony in the pile of what I thought was "bad" luck.

Then another unrecognized break came my way. After reporting to the Auburn University Language Studies Assignment Center, at Auburn, Alabama, I waited in a long line to receive my new orders and became excited when the two privates in front of me were transferred to Queens College for additional training. According to my logic, I'd be sent to Queens too; it was close to home, it was my alma mater, and *that's* where I wanted to go. I had visions of proudly returning home in uniform to greet my classmates, visit my parents, and enjoy some home-cooked meals. But the Army used a different kind of logic, and I was bitterly disappointed. They sent me to what is now Michigan State University at East Lansing for language training. My contingent included a number of German refugees. We all thought that this would be an easy assignment because of our existing language skills, but to our dismay the Colonel in command barked, "You have come here already qualified in a language. Choose another one." For reasons I no longer remember, I chose German. French I would learn later in the European school of romance.

Michigan State wasn't so bad. The campus was devoid of men in civilian clothes as the war removed more and more of them for military service. I had a lovely girlfriend, Audrey Buckner, in Pontiac, and comfortable lodgings in one of the houses on Fraternity Row. Each language group had been assigned to a different house.

And I was able to visit an old classmate, Charles De Bare, at the University of Michigan, 40 or 50 miles away in Ann Arbor. Chuck was involved in the Army's Japanese Language Program there.

For almost six months I was submerged in all things Teutonic at Michigan State, for eight hours a day: German language, conversation, history, geography, and culture. The instruction was thorough, intense, fascinating, and it channeled my boundless energy. When I had attended Queens College, I had worked the 9 p.m. to 1 a.m. shift at Macy's as a stock clerk while taking 30 credits, playing tennis and piano, and participating in war-related organizations such as *Aid To Britain*. I was accustomed to constant activity, and my need for it was well satisfied by the Army training at Michigan State. By Christmas 1943, we were given an extensive written and oral exam and a surprise ten-day furlough. Delighted, I went home.

Getting from Michigan to New York during wartime wasn't easy. The train trip took a day longer than usual, but the uniform often got me a seat and a smile. Trains were packed and the trip meant changing frequently, with long hours of waiting in dreary stations bulging with people. As I read, whining children clung to their mother's hem and the smell of sweat hung everywhere. My duffel bag was a cumbersome nuisance as I tried fitting it between people and seats. Because of the crowding, the cars were unusually hot and stuffy. I managed to open a window and smiles changed to glares as everyone became covered with coal grit.

When I arrived at home, I was delighted to find that my two oldest buddies, Eugene Cahn and Alfred Levin, were also back on leave. But our reunion didn't last long, as I received a telegram ordering me to return immediately. And so I repeated the same miserable travel process in reverse. Back at Michigan State, excited soldiers were waving their arms and yelling, "Franco, hurry up. Get back to your room and pack. We're moving out in an hour."

From Michigan I was sent to McDill Field in Tampa, Florida, and then on to Washington, D.C., where our group was transported by truck in the middle of the night to a well-hidden compound of buildings in Warrenton, Virginia. The next morning I discovered that this was Vint Hill Farms Station, the main quarters of the Signals Intelligence branch of the U.S. Army, later to become the headquarters of the Central Intelligence Agency. I also discovered that I had scored amongst the top ten on the German exam and was sent to Vint Hill to become a cryptanalyst — a *code breaker*.

Even though this work in Europe would keep us out of combat, we were expected to be "true" soldiers at Vint Hill, meaning that we had to be physically prepared for action. To achieve this we were sent on weekly marches. Because most of the men had come from a variety of non-physical backgrounds, they were unfit, and within two miles had to fall out because of blisters and sore muscles. I had had the good fortune of the infantry training, which I had entered as a 5-foot 9-inch, 170-pound, plump, pale Eddie Fisher look-alike. With lousy food and daily physical exertion, I exited as a 140-pound tanned mass of muscle and bone. The 25-mile marches had done the job, and I was grateful.

At Vint Hill our code-breaking training was mostly theoretical and taught us the value of Traffic Analysis (TA), which enabled us to analyze all the information about the message that we knew *before* attempting to break into it. Typically that would include who the sender was, to whom the message was addressed, and the time of sending. For example, the first message sent in the morning was a unit status and requirement report. This would include casualties, ammo status, rations, etc., *and* with typical military beaucratic procedures, these categories were sent in a rigid order. For us, the cryptanalysts, the value of these early morning messages was the code *du jour*, enabling us to crack subsequent messages sent that day. It was like getting the first word of a crossword puzzle. By the time I finished my training, I understood the procedure but seriously doubted my ability to function amidst the pressures and fears of wartime conditions.

◄○►

Regardless of my new-found ability — or inability — April 1944 arrived and our small group of ten was ordered to report for overseas physicals. We waited in the uninviting pale green of institutional unfriend-liness. The chill from our anxiety intensified in the cold barren room as our somber mood seemed to reflect off the sterile walls and the shiny floor. Time ticked and nothing happened. The tension increased as we moved closer to departure and the unknown. We talked. We joked. We bitched.

The door flew open. A medical officer poked his head into the room, glared at us for a moment, and asked, "Is there anyone here with a glass eye?" Our jaws dropped. He slammed the door and departed. That was it. That was our overseas physical exam!

Next we went to see a team of dentists. Mine took one look in my mouth and announced, "You have a bad cavity in one of your rear molars. Sorry, I don't have time to fill it," and with a pair of forceps, yanked out my tooth. I was horrified. Warm liquid filled my mouth; the first taste of wartime blood. I hoped that this would be my only war injury, but I was to be disappointed. Maybe having a glass eye was an advantage!

With every rumor, we imagined a different fate. My usual impatient nature was put to the test waiting for the next challenge. I was itching to move on. At chow that evening one of the clerks nonchalantly leaned toward me and whispered, "You're being flown to London within forty-eight hours."

Fly? Wow! Transatlantic flight was in its infancy, and soldiers shipped overseas were sent by troopships in convoy, not by airplane. Even Churchill had taken a ship a mere three years before when he had sailed to America to meet with Roosevelt. I couldn't believe my good fortune. London! In 48 hours. And by plane! My mind reeled. "I'm twenty years old, an American soldier in a great world war, and in forty-eight hours I'll be in London!" I was awed.

Upon hearing the exciting news of my departure, I decided that secrecy and security be damned and found a public telephone on base, dropped in the coins, and called my folks. Not realizing what an impact such a call from their only child would have upon them, I told them that if they wanted to see me for one last time (a terrible choice of words), they had better "entrain" (my new vocabulary) to Washington immediately.

Their trip was a physical and emotional nightmare as tension mounted and the moment of separation closed in. Since I was restricted to base and they couldn't enter camp, we met at the gate, cold hands pressed against chain-link. Flush with anticipation, I eagerly told them about the great adventure ahead. London. Airplanes. Codes.

For half-an-hour they stood there, sad and subdued with their wisdom of years. Both had lived through World War I on another continent. They knew. My mother smiled bravely, holding back her tears. Trying not to turn around, my parents slowly walked away from the gate at Bolling Field with stiff backs and slumping shoulders. As I watched them leave, the seriousness of my situation hit me, and Rudyard Kipling's poem "The Broken Men" came to mind:

> We took no tearful leaving,
>   We bade no long good-byes . . .
> Ah, God! One sniff of England —
>   To greet our flesh and blood. . . .

I lingered, realizing that this might be the last time I'd ever see them. Too late to say the things I now thought of so clearly, I felt lonely and empty.

To dull my despondency, I searched out the closest Enlisted Mens Club where I got to know a WAC and 3.2 beer, the low-alcohol beverage sold on military bases to reduce drunkenness. I had always disliked the taste of beer but found myself guzzling it to deaden my feelings.

It was not long before the WAC and I found ourselves in a passionate tryst in the middle of the parade grounds with the American Army whistling and cheering us on in good patriotic fashion. I was too excited and too drunk to care. It certainly provided a memorable, albeit hazy, send-off.

Forty-eight hours later, I faced my buddies with a soberness that had nothing to do with alcohol. The excitement and adrenaline of the recent events had carried me toward this moment, but I didn't yet understand what was happening. Naively, I thought I'd soon find out.

Ready for takeoff, I hunched on the hard bench of a brand new four-engine DC-4 transport and reflected upon the circumstances that had taken me through combat training, out of the infantry, and into code-breaking school — events that I could never have predicted or engineered, but that probably saved my life. It was here that I began to feel a sense of destiny as I thought about how these incidents were shaping my future. The wait to take off seemed endless as memories of the past and thoughts of what was to come ran through my head like frames of a movie. The roar of the engines grew louder and the vibration moved through me forcing my jaw to loosen, but the chattering of my teeth continued. We seemed to sit a long time before the two tiny red lights out the window directed the pilot to taxi. A flood of memories created a kaleidoscope of feelings that were ever-changing as the plane gained altitude and banked. I was glad to be here, but I was scared. I looked at my buddy, Teddy Hansen.

———————◀○▶———————

The flight to England was long and tedious and gave me more time to reflect and speculate. On my fifteenth birthday in 1938 the Munich Pact had been signed and Prime Ministers Chamberlain and Daladier sold out their ally and gave Czechoslovakia to Hitler. "Peace in our time" lasted six months. From 1936 on I had wanted to go fight Franco, my namesake across the sea. Because we had shared the same name, I had followed the events in Europe with more than an average interest for someone my age and concluded that the Nazis and Fascists were using Spain as their testing ground and dress rehearsal for what was to come. Never did I dream the actual drama would become so horrific.

Growing up speaking Ladino, the ancient Judeo-Spanish of my father, I developed a keen sense of who I was, but didn't know where I fit. Besides politics, I became absorbed in classical music and English poetry. Too young, I graduated from high school and became a socially inept college freshman. A 16-year-old self-conscious boy is no match for leggy, suntanned, 18-year-old coeds. I was saved from my feelings of social inadequacy by a serious strep infection that killed ten of my classmates at the University of Michigan and sent me home to recover. Later that year when I re-entered college, it was at Queens in my own backyard.

As a child I had always been on the move, impatient with the moment and eager to see around the next corner. After school I'd run in the front door and out the back, *slam-slam*, a one-two punch that told my mother I was home. For hours I would hit the tennis ball against the wall, increasing the speed and allowing the whack of impact to dissolve some of my energy. When I went away to college, I was eager for a new adventure, but didn't understand that I wasn't yet ready for it. In some ways it was similar to my entry into the Army.

In 1942, in the spirit of patriotism and trust, I had enlisted in the Army with the understanding that I would be allowed to complete my education at Queens College before going to war. But unexpectedly, the rules changed and orders were received to report for duty in nine months, leaving me several semesters short of graduation. Although it was understood that the Army could no longer afford to honor its commitment because the need for men was too great, it still left a feeling of betrayal. As I accepted the reality of the situation, I began to see the war as a giant puzzle, and I was one of the pieces. My feelings were mixed. With the intoxication of war and the naiveté of youth, I was eager to fight, but the unknown clutched at my stomach and weakened my knees. Regardless of what I felt, it was out of my hands, and my initial excitement gave way to a slow-growing fear.

During the summer and fall semesters of 1942 I had been given special permission to take 42 credits, but I was still 10 short for graduation. Now I had orders to report to Camp Upton on Long Island and become #12 142 235. For volunteering I got the number "one" added at the front, perhaps a reflection of my IQ for making the decision to join up. "This just isn't fair," I told Harold Lenz, the acting registrar. "I was supposed to get to graduate." He listened to me pour out my frustration before informing me that Queens had recently decided to give 10 credits to students entering the armed forces. *Voilá.* I *would* graduate, *in absentia*, in the June class of 1943 at the age of 19; but no group photo. Death with diploma?

————◄○►————

Engines fired, metal shuddered. The DC-4 turned to taxi. The roar of vibration increased as we lifted off against gravity and ascended into darkness. Convinced we were going down in flames because of the glowing red exhaust escaping from the engines, Teddy Hansen and I sat in terrified silence. My eyes investigated our shivering cocoon. The interior was bare and intimidating, devoid of the soft seats and designer colors that would come later in commercial airliners conveying the silent message, "It's okay. Relax. You'll be fine." Exposed wires lined the walls, running along the equally exposed struts, and the whole thing gave the impression of being held together by chewing gum and Scotch tape. Teddy and I alternated looking out the window, and then at each other, unable or unwilling to speak our thoughts. Even if we had found our voices, the roar of the engines would have swallowed them.

The trip seemed like a surrealistic dream that I couldn't quite grasp. Yet, as apprehensive as I was, this was exactly the kind of life I wanted and thrived on — excitement, adventure, action. But as we took off, I began to realize that I wasn't going to be able to control much of anything for a long time. The name GI was glamorous. The definition *government issue* wasn't. For the first time I understood that I was somebody else's property.

Except for the roar, the plane continued silently through the night. Chins dropped and heads bobbed from shoulder to shoulder as each man dozed or sat absorbed in his thoughts. Fuel and food required a number of stops, allowing us a moment to stretch and gain a bit of confidence as we successfully survived each part of the journey. By the time we arrived in Prestwick, Scotland, after refueling at Newfoundland, Labrador, and Iceland, we had taken off and landed so many times that I felt quite comfortable with flying. In Prestwick we changed to a Douglas DC-3 for the leg to London, where in typical military fashion of "hurry up and wait," nobody was there to pick us up. As soon as we deplaned, I flung my duffel bag down in the middle of the tarmac, stretched out full length with my hands cradling my head, and sighed, "It's good to be here." It was so unusual for my buddies to see me in a state of relaxed immobility that they broke out laughing. I had finally learned what they had known all along — this was "bigger than you; bigger than me; bigger than both of us." In the grand scheme of things, I was only a drop in history's bucket.

Toward the end of a very long day, a truck arrived to transfer us to a British Army base and the evening meal. After a tense and exhausting trip we were eager to sit down, eat, and unwind; but we were to be disappointed. As the long dinner line shortened, the sickening odor of the entrée reached our nostrils, and one by one we dropped out. Mutton and sprouts, a traditional English meal, just wasn't appetizing enough for our growling stomachs. Hungry and tired, we discovered that there was "no room at the inn," a.k.a. barracks, so we laid our heads on our duffel bags and slept outdoors.

The next morning proved to be a beautiful sunny day. Our truck finally arrived and drove us through the rolling green hills of the Buckinghamshire countryside. Charming cottages with colorful gardens dotted the landscape, and memories of my English literature class and Robert Browning's lines came to mind:

> Oh, to be in England
> Now that April's there.
> And whoever wakes in England
> Sees, some morning, unaware, . . .

This precious stone set in the silver sea, . . .
This blessed plot, this earth, this realm,
this England.
— ***King Richard II***, *William Shakespeare*

Chapter Three

Herefords and Haystacks

AH, ENGLAND. In Chalfont St. Giles, a picturesque village near the western outskirts of London, we found our outfit camped at Newlands Park. Assigned to a ten-man tent pitched amidst a herd of wandering Herefords, we were given two instructions, "Watch out for the cow plop, especially at night on your way to the latrine," and "Report to 1st Sergeant Todd."

The 1st Sergeant greeted our arrival with some surprise. "We weren't expecting you so soon. Clean up a bit, and I'll give you a pass to town."

Some of the men were so exhausted that they collapsed onto their cots, but my adrenaline was pumping too fast to relax, and I couldn't wait to get going. I left camp to explore on my own — to get a preview of how I'd spend the next two years searching out every new and unknown adventure.

It was unusually warm as I walked through a Constable-painted landscape and down a winding country lane bordering a small stream where I came upon a charming little cottage and a man busily clipping hedges. I felt a bit like Alice in Wonderland as he asked, "A mite hot today, isn't it Yank? How about a drink?" and called to the house, "Mother, open a couple of beers." Soon we found ourselves sitting around a little table in their yard as if we were old friends.

Leaving these pleasant people, I meandered through a quaint Medieval town with narrow cobbled streets, half-timbered houses, and lovely gardens where I visited John Milton's home. Words from *Paradise Lost* were inscribed over the doorway — words that he had written after going blind. The poem touched me deeply and I reflected upon the last line, "They also serve who only stand and wait," wondering who I had been sent to serve.

As most soldiers tend to do, I eventually found my way to the local pub, The Pheasant, a traditional two-storied building with a hayrack in the courtyard. The place was full of English and American soldiers, English WACS, and Women's Land Army Personnel, the latter actually becoming volunteer farmers for the war's duration. At the bar I was introduced to the local beverages of "Mild and Bitter," a mixture of beer and lager, and "Gin and Orange," which is just what it says. I don't remember where I got the money to pay for the drinks or how long it took before things began to get hazy and very pleasant, but my last recollection was of being in a haystack with a very amenable WLA girl, and a woozy wander back to camp with the scent of hay and perfume lingering upon me. Belly-flopping onto my cot, my last thought was the words of the great bard William Shakespeare:

> This happy breed of men, this little world,
> This precious stone set in the silver sea, . . .
> This blessed plot, this earth, this realm,
> this England.

Oh, what a marvelous country.

————◄○►————

Chalfont St. Giles gave me easy access to London where I had my first exposure to both a European city and the destruction of war. Fortunately I had missed the previous dismal winter when the sun hid itself for six weeks — the kind of weather even the optimists have a tough time smiling about. Lieutenant Mortimer Proctor, Operations Officer of my detachment, related that on one occasion when the sun finally did come out for a brief moment, the people in a local pub ran outside singing "You Are My Sunshine."

The day I visited London was bleak and forlorn. Much of the surrounding countryside was untouched by the devastation, so I was unprepared for what the city brought. Weeds, like forgotten children left standing at attention, grew out of control on lots that once held houses. The space was now empty — a neighborhood forsaken — one that slept underground. I passed block after block of destruction from the German blitz of 1940, all abandoned to futility. I wondered where the people had gone, what they had felt. Every scrap of their identity was lost in one bomb blast. Would they recover? Could they recover?

> It was not part of their blood,
>   It came to them very late
> With long arrears to make good,
>   When the English began to hate. . . .
>
> It was not preached to the crowd,
>   It was not taught by the State.
> No man spoke it aloud,
>   When the English began to hate.
>
> It was not suddenly bred,
>   It will not swiftly abate,
> Through the chill years ahead,
>   When Time shall count from the date
>   That the English began to hate.
>   — Rudyard Kipling

Weeks later, I returned to London on the underground. As I watched from the bleary window, the familiar names of Richmond Hill — where I had been born in New York — and Kew Gardens — a suburb of Queens back home — rushed past in the same geographical alignment as we had back home! It was reassuring to see the same station stops as those in America, and to realize their origin.

Surrounding me in the tube at Hampstead Heath station were the homeless, sleeping in endless rows of tiered bunks and only venturing outside during daylight hours when they thought the German bombers would be at rest, though German bombers rarely flew over London in 1944. The hollow-eyed faces reflected the colorless and monotonous existence that the war had forced them to endure. Objects that helped to pass the time, but provided no identity, could be occasionally seen guarded by the owner — a blanket, a shared book or doll, a pack of cards. Nothing from their life before. Only memories. Could they be the residents of the now vacant neighborhood that I had seen on my last visit to London?

Ascending the stairs into the brisk night air, I found myself engulfed in the notorious London fog and the total vacuum of a blackout. London fog is incomprehensible to those who haven't been sucked into it. Nothing could be seen, not even my hand before me. Exacerbating the condition, all the curtains were drawn and the exterior lights of the city extinguished to protect from the bombers a city that never really slept any more. To find my way, I moved slowly along the buildings, running my hands against the rough stone walls in order to gain some orientation. Street signs were unreadable, and only the perseverance of youth got me through the damp darkness to my destination.

Major Harry Turkel, Commanding Officer of 3rd Radio Squadron Mobile, described in his diary a foggy trip from London back to camp:

> It was hard to see ten feet ahead. The bus is a 2½ ton, snub nosed, prairie schooner vehicle with very hard benches. After an hour of this, someone had to walk and lead the truck. "Even the seagulls are walking," said someone . . . an impenetrable black blanket. I could not see down beyond my hands. One felt rather than saw.

On one occasion, night visibility was reduced to zero and nobody showed up at a local dance except the band and the eager enlisted men. Waiting for the festivities to begin, the fog closed in, prohibiting those in attendance from going home. It was a long disappointing evening, as the men sat around eating ice cream, without any girls.

Occasionally the fog was used to advantage. Waiting for roll call each morning in its cool dampness, radio operator John O'Hara would disappear into it as soon as his name was called and be the first in line for powdered eggs and Spam.

Although I continued to feel the excitement of the war adventure, there were times and places that dragged me down. And Kipling continued to come back to me:

> I long for lustre.
> I am tired of the greys and browns and the
>   leafless ash.
>
> I would have hours that move like a glitter
>   of dancers
> Far from the angry guns that boom and flash.

Private Franco on his first pass from Camp Wheeler, Macon, Georgia, 1943, visiting with his parents, Leon and Emmy Franco.

Milton's Cottage, Chalfont St. Giles, England.

Lieutenant Hugh M. Davidson, Intelligence Officer, Detachment A, 3rd RSM, in Cheadle, England, 1944. Lieutenants Davidson and Proctor were the two most experienced Intelligence officers in Detachment A, 3rd RSM.

The "Crown and Horseshoes" Inn at Langham, Kent, England, a hangout for officers of Detachment B, 1944.

Typical "Limey" vans used by the 3rd RSM; some had been used in the North African campaign. Lieutenant Hugh Davidson, thrown off his cot during a bombardment, landed on the van floor and was covered with sand that sifted out during the shelling.

Sergeants Rohman and Milberg next to the Radio Telephony (R/T) van.

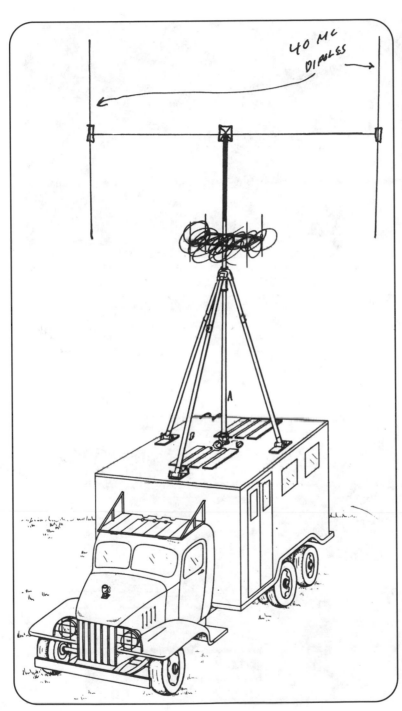

The diagram of changes proposed by Captain Ted Silverstein to improve the operation of the Direction Finding (D/F) van.

Men of Detachment A in Normandy, June-July 1944, taking a break in the shelters built over their foxholes abutting the hedgerow line.

Normandy, July 1944 — Sergeant Eric Scholz deepening his foxhole after the German mine dropping.

Chapter Four

"Flap Able to Easy" 3rd Radio Squadron Mobile (G)

HE 3RD RADIO SQUADRON MOBILE (G) was like a bunch of nomads following the Army. Made up of units that had trained in various geographical locations, we were fighting the same war, but we were fighting it differently.

On April 7, 1944, the 951st Signal Radio Intelligence Company, Aviation, had been reorganized and combined with the newly formed Detachment B and then designated as 3rd American Air Force Radio Squadron, Mobile (G), which was subsequently shortened to 3rd Radio Squadron Mobile (G). 3rd RSM (G) was then assigned to the 9th Air Force, whose code name was "Gangway." Detachment D, of the 3rd RSM, recorded its genesis in its Unit History:

Headquarters detachment of the 3rd Radio Squadron Mobile
(G) had been stationed at a private estate next to the famous
Ascot, England, race track for quite some months and had, with
the aid of manpower supplied from the U.S., progressively
given birth to A, B and C Detachments. On this sunny Saturday
morning, August 12, 1944, Headquarters Detachment evident-
ly was in labor pains again and, lo and behold, at 11 a.m. of this
memorable date brought forth "D" Detachment.

Ultimately the "birth" of the first four detachments would produce 540
officers and enlisted men.

Throughout the testing, training, and transporting of my unit, Detachment A, we were usually kept in the dark as to where we were going and
what we would be doing, and not apprised of the activities of the other
units. Only after we had been operational for some time did we learn that
there were more of "us," just with different names: "Flap" **A**ble, **B**aker,
and **C**harlie, and later **D**og and **E**asy. "Flap" was simply an innocuous
name given that would mean nothing and signify nothing to the enemy.

The primary difference between the units related to the types of communication in which we specialized. Radio Telephony (R/T) — short-
range speech communication — was the job of Detachments B, C, and D.
My group, A, code name Flap Able, was long-range telegraphy, intercepting German Air Force messages of hand-operated Morse known as Wireless (W/T). Because of our long-range ability, we weren't limited to our
own Army as the others were. This provided us with almost constant activity as we were able to pick up transmissions from places as far away as
Norway, the Mediterranean, and the Russian Front where something was
always going on. The limited range of the other detachments kept their
activity restricted to a 200-mile radius, resulting in less radio traffic than
we found.

Some of us had trained in America and others in Europe, many at places
in England like Cheadle — the principal Royal Air Force intercept station
— Middle Valance, Chalfont St. Giles, and Maidstone. Staff Sergeant Bob
Siefert of Detachment B, whose training began in the States and continued
abroad, recalls in his memoirs:

Direction Finding became an interesting pastime on Sunday
afternoons in the city of Fresno [*California*]. We had mobile

equipment mounted on jeeps that would hide behind or among the taller buildings . . ., and we would try to find them. Our first training [*in England*] was experimental to see what would work best. Most messages were very brief and sent quite rapidly and without call letters. You had to be on the ball or you didn't get them.

Earlier in the war, most Intelligence-monitoring stations performing the kind of functions that we were doing were housed in fixed locations with permanently installed antennae. Later, the British campaigns in North Africa showed that the Intelligence squadrons that followed the Army, instead of working from a distance, were more effective. Our outfit was designated as a "Mobile" Radio Squadron because our caravan could move from place to place carrying our radios and collapsible 75-foot antennae. With practice, it took us only a couple of hours to set up for operation and even less time to decamp.

In war, the weather starts at the top of the world. *Westa Eins* (Weather Squadron One), the call letters of a Luftwaffe four-engine Focke-Wulf 200 weather plane, lifted off an airstrip in northernmost Norway each morning at 1 a.m. The plane flew the same course every day, through the same quadrants, sending weather information to German forces.

Also each morning, but two hours later, the FW-200's Allied counterpart took off from a Reykjavik airstrip into skies above Iceland, sending similar information to London. Because the Scandinavian land mass reaches farther to the north than Iceland, our midnight to 8 a.m. shift of intercept operators immediately began copying out the data from the German plane, and almost as quickly, we broke the code. This was because Jerry used the same order of reporting daily — temperature, wind speed, cloud pattern, and so forth — never deviating. The Luftwaffe's strict procedure enabled us to quickly identify the code of the day and break subsequent messages from other German Air Force planes. This is what our training at Vint Hill Farms had been about. By 3 a.m. we were able to break 40 to 50 percent of the messages as soon as they were transmitted, and subsequently relay the information to all detachments. Without the data that the German weather planes provided, we would have had a great deal more trouble and delay.

Official records of 3rd RSM regarding Detachments B, C, and D state that:

Voice intercept was able to pick up and intercept an enemy message, locate an enemy ground station or aircraft, discover the intention of such aircraft, and transmit this information to a fighter control center normally within 40 to 50 seconds. The number of messages passed to TAC [Tactical Air Command] on a typical active day [was] approximately 200 and relates almost entirely to the presence of German day fighters.

————◄o►————

Throughout the war there were many colorful characters that crossed our path, and although I never had the pleasure of meeting the legendary Brigadier General Elwood "Pete" Quesada, called "the innovator of modern tactical warfare," Bob Siefert did during his training in England. General Quesada, of the Tactical Air Command, of the 9th Air Force, who embodied the American "can do" spirit, had the look of a Spanish conquistador, and what I had heard about him made me think that he was the 9th's most effective General. A daring fighter pilot, he spent his off-duty hours making cabinets and women. With the latter he took along men from his unit to share his bachelor activities. In one of his letters home, he asked for a monthly supply of stockings and lipstick. Instead, mom sent chapstick and mens socks. That ended his requests.

Unexpectedly, Quesada showed up at Detachment B with other top brass for a surprise inspection. Captain Ted Silverstein, the detachment's Commander, had been away all day gathering equipment and had left his adjutant, Lieutenant Jim Copp, in charge. It was a heady time for a young officer to find himself faced with Major General Yount, head of the Training Command of the U.S. Army Air Forces; General Dwight D. Eisenhower, Commander-in-Chief of Supreme Headquarters Allied Expeditionary Forces (SHAEF); and Brigadier General Pete Quesada. Most of the detachment's equipment and forward personnel were already on their way to the beachhead for the Normandy invasion, so there was very little of interest to show them. Fortunately for Copp, Captain Silverstein returned and conducted a "talking inspection." When there was nothing left to say, the officers prepared to leave. As Silverstein stood at attention, Quesada asked, "How's the drainage here, Captain?"

"Drainage?" thought Silverstein. For a moment he was flustered trying to figure out what he had forgotten.

With a twinkle in his eye, Quesada remarked, "We'll try it," and the entire party unzipped their pants and urinated over the hedgerows. To everyone's relief the drainage was just fine.

Impressing the brass was always a challenge — one that Lieutenant Ferdinand (Fred) Gottlieb, Commander of Detachment D, didn't relish when he was informed that the bigwigs were arriving, wanting to see what *his* outfit was doing. He had been told to put on a show for the inspection, but there was hardly any air traffic and therefore very few transmissions. He alerted his men to the situation, and as soon as the officers arrived, everyone began fiddling with the dials, adjusting their earphones, and looking busy. When the visitors asked what the "transmissions" were saying, the radio operators explained that German planes were flying over a certain area and that their messages were being forwarded on to Head-quarters. This news produced handshaking, back-slapping, and picture taking.

Although I missed out on meeting General Quesada, I was fortunate enough to encounter another "celebrity," former British rugby player Wing Commander G. Rowley Scott-Farnie, during my training at Chalfont St. Giles. Along with the brilliant mastermind and trickster Reginald Victor (R. V.) Jones, head of Scientific Intelligence on Britain's Air Staff who was considered to be the father of electronic warfare, Scott-Farnie helped figure out how to pick up the German radio beams (code name "Head-aches") that guided the Jerry pilots to their targets; and he devised a plan (code name "Aspirin") to move the beams. This tricked the enemy into dropping bombs on empty fields instead of populated areas. In his warm friendly manner, Scott-Farnie would look over my shoulder and encourage me with a "Oh, jolly good old chap. That's very good." The American offi-cers loved him and his Squadron Leader, S/L Waters, affectionately called Sugar/Love Waters by Lieutenant Hugh Davidson, my superior officer.

One day I was having some difficulty with a code as Scott-Farnie made his daily rounds. The British officer in charge told him of the problem. Scott-Farnie hesitated only a moment. "Oh, yes, we're having a problem with it too, but in a couple of days I'll get it solved." And he did. I learned later that he had sent a commando unit to a German radar station on the coast of France and within three days obtained the code that we needed.

This was astounding to me! I felt my eyes grow as large as a little boy's watching a chocolate bar wave before him. The fact that Scott-Farnie had the power to say, "Hey, I want this thing," and then order men to go and get it, was extremely impressive to a very green Buck Private fresh from the States. The Germans have a word for it — *zeitgeist* — the spirit of the times, the spirit of the person.

Scott-Farnie was impressed with *us*, too, and on October 31, 1944, wrote a letter of commendation to SHAEF about 3rd RSM:

> It is safe to say that no results comparable with these have ever been achieved before by a field "Y" unit and is due to the enthusiastic manner in which the IXth Air Force have employed their "Y" resources. On many occasions [Fighter] Squadrons have been held at readiness to operate solely on "Y" information. The results speak for themselves.

Many operational men like myself received the bulk of our training in England directly from the British, practicing on live, "in the moment," German broadcasts. Working closely with the English allowed us to share messages that might have been missed due to unpredictable weather conditions, which produced static and unreliable radio reception. This constant exchange of critical information enabled us to respond quickly and effectively. Without the continual cooperation of the British Signals Intelligence, the code war could never have been won so quickly. When Admiral Walter Anderson, one of the Navy brass, was asked about the importance of wartime code breaking he replied, "It won the war."

Although the Brits had better code-breaking skills than we did, because of their previous four-year war experience, we still felt that our work excelled because of our effective use of German refugees, some of whom were Jewish, which aided our ability to interpret quickly and correctly. The Brits, however, did not employ them in their code-breaking units for fear that Nazis might have been planted amongst them. In addition, they disdained what they called the "bad form" of the refugees, who would enthusiastically — and very "unmilitarily" — jump up and down and clap whenever a German plane was hit. But there were exceptions. Lieutenant Peter White recounts that the British would occasionally acquiesce and use a refugee entertainer to imitate the voice of the enemy flight controller and give contrary instructions to German pilots, thereby creating mass confusion for Jerry.

The enemy sent two levels of secret transmissions. Anything encrypted in the high-grade code of their complex Enigma machine was termed by the British "TOP SECRET ULTRA" or simply ULTRA — sometimes referred to as "Source." Being untrained and unequipped to break this highly sophisticated code, we relayed it directly to the British at Bletchley Park, near London, the only place where ULTRA could be decoded. Two-and-a-half hours after the Germans sent their "unbreakable" ULTRA messages, the codes were broken. Because it was vital that the Germans not know that the Allies were capable of doing this, strict orders were given forbidding any action to be taken on these transmissions until the British had time to determine what response, if any, should occur. General Quesada cautioned his men about reacting to ULTRA: "If you use this the wrong way, you'll get your ass kicked out of the theater" — meaning the whole war. This didn't mean that the officers in charge weren't allowed to devise plans and give orders, it just meant that all military action based on ULTRA information had to be cleverly masked to protect the source.

Only a couple of dozen men knew of the existence of ULTRA, and at 9th Air Force it was Generals Hoyt S. Vandenberg and Robert Lee who received the daily briefings. On one occasion a message was received pinpointing the exact location of German tanks hiding in the forest. Knowing that a direct attack would alert Jerry as to the source of the Allies' information, planes were sent to bomb a number of different targets. Success in "accidentally" hitting the tanks accomplished the mission and maintained complete secrecy. That was the way you had to work with ULTRA — pretend you didn't know.

Low-grade code, however, was *our* "stuff" and, unlike ULTRA, could be broken and acted upon immediately. Using the information that was received based on Y (Wireless), the 9th Air Force predicted "Operation Goldrigen." While the British were caught napping, 400 to 500 German fighter bombers attacked the Allied airfields in Belgium and France on New Year's Day 1945, inflicting heavy losses upon the planes caught on the ground. With the aid of Y Intelligence, the American Generals had been able to alert the 9th Air Force fighter squadrons, sending their planes aloft before the attack and thereby minimizing our losses.

Assisting us was a code book of approximately 1,000 sequence-numbered items — and our intuition. To simplify our work we used universal "Q" codes that allowed us to respond quickly to one another without having to go through the laborious and time-consuming effort of sending entire words or messages. Because brevity in code breaking was essential, the following Q codes were frequently used:

QRB: Your message regarding broadcast received and under-
        stood.
QRM: Static.
QRU: I have nothing for you.
QTP: Accept my priority message at once.
QUO: I am forced to stop transmitting owing to imminent dan-
        ger. If possible, I will try to make contact with you on
        my next schedule.
QRV: I am ready.

Guessing was also valuable and often brought impressive results, as I was to learn later.

————◄○►————

My code-breaking work tools were pencil and paper put to use when radio operators came through the door bearing sheaves of enemy messages from the Wireless container-trailer. The procedure we followed was simple. The six to eight radios with their operators in the radio van would constantly monitor various assigned radio frequencies that they knew the Germans used. Each radioman would fiddle with the dials until he hit the frequency where he heard either Morse Code or a pilot's voice. This mes- sage would then be sent to the D/F (Direction Finding) wagons, where two nails and a string were used to determine the triangulation and get a fix on location, and then to our wagon where the four-man teams of cryptan- alysts, of which I was one, went to work to "break" (decode) these messages into plain German text. The German was then translated into English and sent to various Headquarters of the 9th Air Force, to SHAEF, to RAF Headquarters at Cheadle, and to other interested parties. The Inter- cept, Direction Finding, and Intelligence vans were connected to each other by telephones, and the Intelligence van relied on motorcycle mes- sengers and direct land lines to deliver the "breaks" in order to avoid our messages being intercepted by the Germans.

The Intelligence vans of Detachment B were known as "Rumor" and "Gossip." These cream-colored windowless containers on wheels, typical of those in other detachments, were smaller than the trailer of a large over-the-road semi and furnished with a central table on which all information was correlated and smaller tables along the periphery. Situation maps papered the walls, and "Rumor" was additionally decorated with a swastika each time a German plane was destroyed.

The operating personnel — those responsible for radio interception, direction finding, and code breaking — remained enlisted men throughout the war, but even though our promotions were limited, we did develop a close relationship with our officers because of the nature of our work and the amount of time spent together waiting for German activity to begin. Because of this, strict military behavior was seldom followed; however, authority was understood and respected.

The high level of intelligence and education of this small group gave us common ground to share music, literature, and ideas with our superiors, generating long, intense, and stimulating discussions. One night while Lieutenant Proctor was listening to the radio, I remarked, "That sounds like Brahms Double Concerto." Surprised, he stopped and nodded, "You know that?"

Usually our work was quiet work. We would sit with no one saying a thing, then, suddenly, it all broke loose. Occasionally a lull would generate creativity. During one of these times, a Duty Officer from Detachment A anonymously wrote a poem about my group. Using code, he described the four shifts, the three enlisted men assigned to each shift, how we acted when messages came in, and the spirit of the time. Its title is indicative of the moment:

15 MINUTES OF SPARE THOUGHTS
Met 1
(A Poem in Code)

The D.O.'s are fairy'd at times
By super G.A.F. call signs.
Many a night we find "A" sign
Coded in plenty of time.

Westa often drifts a little west,
But Lynch sez it's southwest.
Be damned sez Teets. It's northwest.
Replies Phelps, make it the best.

Now Rosenberg hovers like a hawk
Over fuck-up messages that are brought.
Franco hollers, I'll be damned, if it's not so.
What can poor Irish do but shout?

Tis Wein we have in mind
When Powell asks the time.
Paris may be off the beaten line,
It's Hansen there every time.

Take a number from one to three.
Reeves yells, Auggy, I'll three.
Old Weiss is right back up a tree.
Go to lunch you bastards — without me!

Now take this big man Small
He makes a switchboard for them all.
Sez maintenance is always on the Ball,
But that's not what I heard about Small.

"Met 1," the poem's title, refers to the code breakers; G.A.F. the German Air Force. "A" is Detachment A. My group, the Intelligence unit of Detachment A, consisted of ten officers and twelve enlisted men, nine of whom had recently arrived with me. Eight-hour "tricks" (shifts) were worked around the clock. The groups of three enlisted men serving together were Lynch, Teets, and Phelps; Rosenberg, Franco, and Irish; Wein, Powell, and Hansen; and Reeves, Augustynowycz, and Weiss.

The Duty Officer's (D.O.) poem was not a great literary masterpiece, but certainly a fun remembrance. Someone was always ready to create mischief in Detachment A, whether it be on paper or through practical jokes. Occasionally, an operator would drift off to sleep during a slow time, only to be awakened by the heat of burning matches stuck into the soles of his boots.

Unlike those of us in Detachment A who waited for the paperwork to arrive before our work really began, the radio operators were always on the alert. We had great admiration for these men who developed the ability to identify the sender and his location after hearing only a few Morse Code dits and dahs. This "signature," known as radio finger painting, was as individualized as fingerprints. Because an intercept operator couldn't very well ask the enemy to repeat his message, he had to hone his skills, and get it right the first time. It was a tough feat because the signals, overlaid with static, would fade in and out. This demand for never-ending concentration created tension that was draining and nerve wracking.

Sergeant John O'Hara, trained in Morse Code, had graduated third in a class of 600 and had attained the incredible speed of 25 words per minute, a speed that could only be increased by the use of a typewriter. During one of his tricks, he received a radio message that was so loud it blew the headset off his ears and threw him off his chair. Fearing the possibility of more pain and a permanent hearing loss, O'Hara was never again able to relax while on duty.

Although 3rd RSM was made up primarily of Southerners, the radio Intelligence section of Detachment A was mostly Northerners, with the exception of a few Californians.

The Commanding Officer of Detachment A, Captain William Brinson, was a Georgian. A short, bandy man with the air of a Southern plantation owner, he walked with a bounce that planted each foot firmly in place as he surveyed his men and his territory. He was wise enough to leave the running of the Intelligence section of the Detachment in the capable hands of his Operation Officers, Lieutenants Mortimer Proctor, son of the governor and namesake of the town of Proctor, Vermont, and a Yale graduate, and Hugh Davidson, a University of Chicago alum who later became a professor of French literature. Proctor was a man with slightly bulging eyes and protruding ears that framed a ruddy friendly face. His medium height and light hair matched Davidson's, except that Davidson was of slight build with a sallow complexion and even handsome features. Always neatly dressed regardless of conditions, Davidson is remembered by Brinson as a ". . . many splendored officer. He answered to no one." Both Davidson and Proctor had been cryptanalysts with the State Department before enlisting and left me with vivid memories of their intelligence and abilities.

The overall Commander of the squadron was Major Harry Raymond Turkel, a master and a mystery because of his dual duties as both Commander of 3rd RSM and Signal Intelligence Officer of 9th Air Force. He was a tall, but slightly stooped man who wore a thin mustache on a dark exotic face, which added to his mystique. A man of great energy and daring, he was driven and was a driver of his subordinates, who both admired and feared him. Because of the diverse responsibilities that caused him to "disappear," even his Executive Officer, Lieutenant William Shaughnessy, frequently didn't know his whereabouts. A Harvard Law School graduate who spoke six languages, it was Turkel's proficiency in German that got him assigned to secret missions arresting enemy VIPs and negotiating armistices, as he did with the surrender of Cherbourg.

Turkel's initial task in England had been to select the personnel to form 3rd RSM (G) in an incredibly short two months. In order to accomplish this in the time allotted, he used the "Lusty Letter," his carte blanche from the government, to do whatever he wanted to expedite the mission. This was how First Lieutenants Bill Shaughnessy and Jim Copp came to be under his command.

One day while walking through camp with Shaughnessy, Copp was stopped by a soldier. "Copp?"

"Yup," Jim answered.

"I think I know you. My name's Greenberg. I remember you from Harvard. If you're looking for a job, come on over to the office, and I'll see what I can do."

So they went, and he told them about some crazy nut — Turkel — running all over London looking for people to work with him on some stuff. "He's a very secret guy, and he might be dropping behind enemy lines," Greenberg added.

That wasn't very appealing, but Copp and Shaughnessy were ready to pursue anything that would get them away from camp because as "casuals," they had no assigned duties and were going stir crazy from boredom. They agreed to meet Turkel.

"Casuals" were the leftovers, the excess men. In this case, 700 men had been mistakenly sent to fill a request for 70, so Copp and Shaughnessy became part of the unneeded 630. Typical. When we really needed something, we found it impossible to get; but when we didn't need it, the Army produced "casuals." Maybe a better word would have been "casualties."

Greenberg cut their orders, and they boarded the train for London. After checking into the Cumberland Hotel, close to the American Embassy in Grosvenor Square, they went to see the Major. Waiting in a little anteroom of an imposing residence, they were greeted by a slim, stern gentleman who snapped, "One at a time," and escorted Copp into his office.

"This is not about dropping behind enemy lines," he explained, "but it is highly secretive work that I can't tell you about at the moment . . . it'll take you into the assault forces of the invasion. Are you willing to do that?" With a lump in his throat, Copp answered "yes," having no idea what he was agreeing to do. He also didn't know at the time that Turkel had read his dossier and discovered that both he and Turkel had attended Los Angeles High School, Stanford, and Harvard.

Turkel needed men who knew something about military procedure because he had been commissioned straight out of the State Department as a volunteer and had no military background other than six weeks training to learn the courtesies of the service. Before being sent to Europe, he had gone first to Africa as an officer in the Air Transport Command (ATC) and then to England.

After the interviews, he readily accepted both Copp and Shaugnessy, but they didn't find out what they had agreed to do until later, when they received their clearance. Eventually it was explained that they would be intercepting German communication — "Voice," as the British called it, and W/T, Wireless Telegraph.

Staff Sergeant Kurt Tannenwald remembers that he was questioned by Major Turkel for two full days before being chosen. As one of the German-born American soldiers, he was at a premium because of his language skills. For training he was sent to Sutton Valance, a farm with "an antenna sticking out of every haystack." There he found learning very difficult because the RAF teacher, Lieutenant Gough, was a pretty young woman who made concentrating on the "right" things a major challenge.

For the two new Lieutenants under Turkel's direct command, there were problems of a different nature. Shaughnessy had been trained in radar, and Copp also had a Signal Corps background, a much different kind of work than that for which they were now being recruited. Their first assignment with Turkel sent them to 9th Air Force Headquarters at Ascot, the site of the famous horse races. This location had created a logistical nightmare at the train station because of the hordes of people going to the track, and it did nothing for military public relations when soldiers were moved to the front of the line, past the disgusted mutterings of, "Those yanks!"

Because Shaughnessy and Copp were ground people — Army people — they were perplexed about being assigned to the Air Corps. In Ascot they were given a little office above the stables of a manor house that was owned by the Crown and Prince Philip, who was into trotters. Later, Shaughnessy became Turkel's Executive Officer, and Copp was assigned to assist Captain Silverstein in forming Detachment B by draining men from other units — primarily the German-speaking Americans like Tannenwald who possessed the ability to hear accents during interception that the American German-speaking radio operators had difficulty distinguishing.

In addition to Shaughnessy and Copp being confused about their assignment, Lieutenant Proctor's diary also reflects his bewilderment regarding operations:

> Gangway [the code name for the 9th Air Force], . . . represents all headquarters in its confused state. . . . No one there knows where anyone is; no one has a proper job to do. They have Hq's at Ascot, at Grandcamp, and now St. Savene — Rear Headquarters, Headquarters and Advanced Headquarters respectively, and between the three affairs go sour very quickly. A matter arising here will be something quite different by the time it gets to Ascot.

——————◄○►——————

Although confusion occasionally reigned, and life around us appeared to be ordered chaos, we performed well. We were a diverse outfit that sometimes created its own problems, but we understood the objective and did our best to accomplish it. Fingers can always be pointed at mistakes, but as our CO Captain Brinson put it, "We won that war in spite of our errors." And winning is what it was all about.

——————◄○►——————

The war changed men's lives because of brilliance, stupidity, absurdity, and luck. I was experiencing all of it.

Chapter Five

The Enemy Within

ERE I SIT upon my chair,
Catching static from the air.
I'm bored to death, I'm going crazy,
And though I'm only 23, already my vision's hazy.

When the armistice comes, and then my leave,
To forsake this prison without reprieve.
I'll swim the ocean if I must,
I'll make the U.S.A. or bust.
— By a poor R/T slave

There were many enemies within, and the military understood
them well. Boredom, a dangerous commodity, left time to think, and

thinking produced homesickness, mutiny, desertion, and even violence. It allowed time to understand the idiocy of war. Days were spent in anticipation, excitement, disappointment, and monotony. We would move from periods of comparative tranquillity to times of trial and transit.

Because camp life for many of the units was tedious and dull, Mail Call became a main event — a welcome diversion. Mail was important to every GI, and letters were read repeatedly for something to do, and to keep alive memories of home. When I first arrived overseas I wrote frequently, and couldn't understand why my folks were ignoring my questions. Later I learned that besides censorship, they hadn't received any of the letters I had written during my first six weeks of overseas duty. General Eisenhower had issued secret orders to hold all mail from England to prevent security leaks that might imperil the invasion of Europe. My mother had become so distraught she had bombarded the War Department with calls and letters, but to no avail. When my letters finally did arrive, the ones I had written from Normandy after the invasion preceded those I had written earlier in England.

Once we had arrived in Europe, all our mail had to be written on special "V-mail" stationery, which was censored, microfilmed, and then sent Stateside, sometimes with large sections cut out. This censorship prevented my family from receiving any specific information from me, and sometimes caused them also to keep asking the same questions. But I was grateful for anything addressed to APO 696 with my name on it.

One afternoon I was so engrossed in reading a letter on the way to the latrine, the unreliable information center of the U.S. Army, that I almost didn't get there. The news was so shocking it stopped me cold. I was going to be a brother! At the age of 21 my parents took away my only-child status and were replacing me with a baby. For some reason I was embarrassed. Maybe at that age I didn't think that my "old" fortyish folks were still having sex!

Corporal Mike Palumbo, a Direction Finding Operator from Detachment B, used the mail to let off steam by sending letters to his grandmother containing the foulest four-letter language imaginable. Always pushing the limits, it was never known if his letters were a joke, if he was trying to shock the censor, or if he even had a grandmother.

As censor of 3rd RSM, Squadron Leader Major Harry Turkel was able to write anything he wanted, but couched his messages in charming stories sent to his infant son and four-year-old daughter:

Dear Marg Anne and William,

September 30, 1944 — [Daddy's] carbine is called Sawtooth because the stock is so notched up with all the Jerries Daddy thinks he got.

October 26, 1944 — Next to knocking off a Naz-eye, your Daddy loves to kill a bottle or two of strong French grape juice.

November 20, 1944 — In Holland . . . Daddy is fighting off the cold. . . . Daddy suffered, but don't go wasting any pity on the old man — HE never sleeps in a pup tent in the snow. Daddy's command car has side curtains and is going to have a home-made heater. Daddy always carries a big thermos bottle of coffee . . . but he shivers so much that [he] never get[s] more than half a cup. . . . Your Daddy carries some cough syrup which goes by the odd name of Vat 69. Daddy has been smoking too many free cigarettes. He is going to be very strong-minded and cut down on his smoking as soon as the ration is reduced to one pack a week.

In addition to mail to provide distraction, on October 9, 1944, we had the experience of voting in the presidential election — some of us for the first time. Because of the vast number of soldiers in Europe, Congress passed a law providing for absentee ballots. For some reason the Army was concerned that it would be accused of making this difficult for us, so postcards were handed out for each man to sign showing that he had received a ballot. As the noncom responsible for passing out the cards in his unit, Staff Sergeant Henry Schueftan encountered some guys in Detachment B who were very unenthusiastic about the event. One soldier refused. "I don't care if you vote or not," declared a disgusted Schueftan, "just sign the damn card to show that you got the ballot and then do whatever you want." Apparently the obstinate man was in the minority because the final tally showed that 60 percent of us voted.

Fortunately my duties kept me busy most of the time, and being the fastest typist, I had the privilege of preparing the daily reports, and therefore getting to know what was going on throughout the squadron before sending it on to Headquarters. But for others, boredom became a major enemy.

Keeping a group of raging hormones in check was a military challenge as the monotony increased and tension mounted. Evenings were particularly difficult, not knowing what to do after all the magazines had been read, the letters written, and the movies seen: *Back to Bataan*, *The Strange Affair of Uncle Henry*, *The Lady on the Train*, and *Junior Miss*. Pinochle, Poker, and Hearts were played for a penny a point with matchstick chips, and the players settled up on pay day, with very little money changing hands.

Besides activities within camp, we were entertained at village dances with the local girls and USO shows. Bob Hope entertained the troops at High Wycombe, and Katherine Cornell starred in *The Barretts of Wimpole Street* in Rheims. As part of one of the shows, Mickey Rooney was assigned to Detachment B for meals and was well-liked by the men, but Joe Louis on the other hand, proved to be a better fighter than he was a comedian. Lieutenant Copp, a nightclub entertainer in civilian life remarked, "He really couldn't tell jokes at all." Just because you can throw a punch doesn't mean you can throw a punch line.

Perhaps Copp would have been better received than Louis, who according to Lieutenant Peter White, ". . . conducted himself as an officer flawlessly . . . [with] excellent manners that greatly impressed the European aristocrats who accepted him as one of their own. He was a handsome man who stood out — one you didn't forget." His charismatic personality that had made him such a successful entertainer before the war, also made him popular with his men.

Occasionally we had slow times that produced some memorable stories like the one Private 1st Class Teplinsky wrote for the July 1944 Unit History of Detachment B:

> I had just finished supper and decided to take a short walk to break the monotony of camp life. The sun had begun to drop from it's [sic] perch in the sky, and the coolness of this warm day made me feel good. A day in Normandy without rain was a rare thing. . . . I noticed some kids playing on the grass near a shell torn cottage. One of them wore a pair of German boots that came up well past his knees. The others were dressed in GI clothing, from shoes to a sun tan shirt sporting a set of sergeant stripes. . . . One called out, "Bonbons monsieur?". . . I noticed that all of them were smoking cigarettes.

. . . An old woman came trudging along, leading a mule laboring heavily under his burden of loaded milk cans. The woman wore a long dusty black dress, and kept her eyes fastened to the ground. . . . Usually the French would say "Bonjour". . . but here was a woman who said nothing. . . . I entered the town . . . [that] resembled an unused motion picture set in Hollywood. The stillness of this deathly quiet scene was broken for a moment when a pack of yapping dogs dashed out into the road after a hapless cat. The noise faded, and there was silence once more. . . . There was nothing. No people, no music, no laughter. Undoubtedly fears of war and enslavement had altered all of that and placed the town under a blanket of silence. . . . A sudden shout reached my ears, and a band of children dashed out . . . singing the ["Marseillaise"] and waving a [tricolor] flag of the French republic. "Americain, Americain," . . . They raised two fingers in the victory salute. . . . My heart beat faster. I thought to myself "That [old woman] is the France of yesterday and . . . [the children are] the France of tomorrow."

. . . As I walked along the road back to camp, I saw the old woman and her mule. The milk cans had been taken from his back, and without his burden, the animal seemed to skip blithely along, hee hawing at irregular intervals. The old woman was humming a tune, and she no longer kept her eyes glued to the ground. She noticed me this time and said, "Bonjour monsieur."

. . . "Yes," I said to myself, "France is coming back to life after a long sleep. When the burden is lifted from the rest of this occupied country, everyone will hum and skip, just like the old woman and her mule."

At each campsite there was usually a town or pub nearby to practice our French language and our American charm. Sometimes a game of basketball or soccer was organized with the civilians, occasionally accompanied by champagne toasts, bouquets, and speeches. Cigarettes, fruit, and chewing gum were our prize contributions.

We frequently passed the time at local farmhouses where the proprietors sold a regional drink. These places were wistfully known as bars, although they far from resembled such establishments. The more elaborate ones might consist of a table or two under a tree where a soldier could pretend he was on holiday as the liquor led his mind into illusion.

Tall, lanky, morose Private Day got himself into big trouble in one of these places. He wandered in, threatening to shoot everyone. In retaliation, they wanted to shoot him. By the time the story reached Captain Silverstein, the officer in charge, the locals had embellished it saying that Day had come in and tried to rape all the inhabitants. Realizing that this was rubbish, Silverstein calmed everyone down by scheduling a trial. Following the formalities of a court-martial, Day was sentenced to a week's latrine duty. This appeased the locals and pleased Private Day because the company moved out two days later, considerably shortening his sentence. After the incident he came to see Lieutenant Copp in the Orderly Room. "Well, Sir, ever since my mammy burned up, I've been kind of funny." Copp dropped the subject.

Alcohol created a lot of problems and almost got me killed. Detachment A was an ethnic rainbow of men that included three friendly American Indians — friendly as long as they stayed away from the local firewater that transformed them into Mr. Hydes. One night while on guard duty at the edge of camp, I heard a rustling in the hedgerow and turned quickly just as an Oglala Sioux shoved a Tommy gun into my gut.

"I'm going to kill you," he said in a cold, quiet alcohol-ladened voice.

Incredulously I said, "Henry, what are you doing?"

He continued threatening and I realized that he wasn't joking. Thinking I could distract him, I suggested, "Why don't we smoke a peace pipe?"

With a glazed stare, he poked me again with the end of the barrel. As we faced off, two guys from my unit emerged from the forest, grabbed him from behind, and took his gun. They had been drinking together at a local farmhouse in Cricqueville and had become increasingly uncomfortable as they watched the Indian get drunk on raw Calvados, a French rotgut concoction, somewhat reminiscent of whiskey, made from 40 percent gasoline, 50 percent alcohol, and 10 percent impurities. From experience, they were concerned about what might happen, and had slipped the ammo clip out of his weapon and followed him back to camp. What they didn't know was whether or not there was still a live round in the chamber. At first I was simply relieved to have been rescued, but as the realization of the event took hold, my stomach tightened.

After my next encounter with the "enemy within," I was much more cavalier about it. "Frenchy," a radio operator from Maine, with French heritage, was nonchalantly cleaning and checking his carbine on his way to the radio caravan to begin his trick. It was Standard Operating Procedure — SOP — to carry weapons at all times; however, they weren't supposed to be loaded except when we were on guard duty. As I was leaving the Intelligence caravan, Frenchy was checking his gun by following the SOP. He pulled back the bolt and squeezed the trigger. Not expecting a bullet in the chamber, he neglected to fire into the air and the bullet whizzed within inches of my ear. Everybody stopped for a moment to see where the shot had come from and then continued on their way.

The war changed men's lives because of brilliance, stupidity, absurdity, and luck. I was experiencing all of it.

——————◄◌►——————

Our superiors did what they could to provide activities for diversion, but the continual repetition of our tasks and the unusual amount of detail it took to keep our camp in smooth working order created a persecution complex among some of the men. A small group felt that they were unjustly treated by being made to work in their spare time, so Captain Silverstein of Detachment B addressed the problem by holding an open gripe session. The men were allowed to let off steam and air their views in front of the officers without fear of retaliation. As the men stood in formation under the Norman apple trees, Silverstein gave full rein to "let it fly." When the men had exhausted their frustration, he vented his.

> What the devil do you men want? Do you want to go home? Do you want someone's shoulder to cry on and have your heads tenderly patted? Whenever I look at any of you, your faces are so long that it makes me feel rotten too. The trouble with all of you is that you are too busy feeling sorry for yourselves to realize that what you are doing is for your own benefit. You holler about latrines. Would you rather straddle slit trenches? If you can do that, so can I. Can't you see that while you are on these details, you are merely constructing devices for your own convenience?

Silverstein stopped, looked at every man individually, and waited. The silence could be felt as each man stood rigid. When no one answered he said, "Well, are there any more gripes?" Again silence.

> Very well, from now on let's not see any more long faces around here. When you see someone, say hello. A little cheery smile will go a long way and make everything look better; your day will be off to a flying start.

The men were dismissed. Some smiled, some groaned, some did nothing; but the following days proved that the CO's talk had taken root, as the men went quietly about their duties.

————◄○►————

We seldom left camp, and thus anything to break the monotony was welcome. For some, alcohol helped. For others, nothing did. Sometimes our marches offered welcome respite and unusual observations of the local people. One of these marches provided me with my own "old woman" story. We were moving along both sides of a dirt road as was customary, to keep the middle open for vehicles, when a dark-cloaked figure approached down the center. As it shuffled nearer I was able to identify an old woman. Seemingly oblivious to her surroundings, she moved closer as we marched past. Her head was wrapped in a tattered shawl framing a deeply lined leathery face. About a hundred yards from me she stopped. Lifting up her dusty ankle-length black dress, she squatted. When finished, she straightened herself up, brushed off her skirt, and continued on. We just kept marching.

One of our favorite diversions in the ever-present sameness was the local dances. They were organized by the townsfolk and gave them a feeling of contributing to the war effort. These events were supposed to relieve pent-up tension, but unfortunately the dance in Pargny les Reims turned into an ethnic free-for-all that put the town off-limits. The residents had organized the event in a cavernous building with nothing more to offer than a high ceiling and a swept floor. I was dancing with a French girl when she grabbed my arm and whispered, "Quick, let's get out of here," as she pulled me out the door. Mistaking her intent, I eagerly agreed before noticing the commotion going on behind us. One of the Southerners in my detachment had gotten ticked off because a black soldier was dancing with a white girl. He began pushing and yelling obscenities. Suddenly the room exploded with men slugging at each other and the blacks going after everyone white. We ran into a neighboring barn and up to the loft where we hid behind bales of hay, listening to the ruckus until the MPs arrived. The Negro battalion, being in the majority, beat up a lot of the Southern boys, and being one of the white boys I would have been one of the unlucky if I had stayed. Obviously the American Army was not happy when we returned to camp. After that incident the blacks and whites were given passes to town on alternate nights.

The diversity that composed all of 3rd RSM created problems within itself. There was an unusual difference in backgrounds, intelligence, education, and race. Some of the substrata of support personnel particularly were troublesome, appearing to resent what they interpreted to be privileges for others, like the code breakers. Unable to understand the reasons and mechanics of war, they were jealous of the men of the Intelligence unit who seemed to have a softer life. Could this have been the reason we code breakers of Detachment A were never promoted more than the "ordinary GIs" — to possibly keep "peace in the family"?

Looking back, I can see that it didn't matter that we wore the same uniform or that we were fighting a common goal. All that some could see was the prejudice they had lived with. We even saw it in England. The British disliked the Chinese Americans but accepted the blacks. It was absurd. We were in Europe fighting a war because of prejudice and at the same time beating each other up for the same reason. Dissension and prejudice needed no antagonist from Germany. The enemy from within was alive and well.

The Normandy invasion had three prerequisites for its success: command of the sea, command of the air, and dispersal of the German ground forces.

Chapter Six

The Great Collaboration

OR ALMOST TWO YEARS, every detail of the Normandy invasion had been planned, to create a moment in history, June 6, 1944, never to be forgotten. As May drew to an end, the U.S. Army's anti-tank battalion of the 30th Infantry Division, camped in the field next to us at Chalfont, began moving out, creating a pervasive dusty cloud. Columns of canvas-covered trucks rumbled down the roads jammed with helmeted men hunched forward on rifles tucked tightly between their knees. Many would never be seen again.

As the week passed, the tension grew with the excitement and dread of the unknown. We were a bunch of young, anxious recruits ready to see some action and envious of those who had been ordered to move out, leaving us behind. Although our duties required us to follow the Army, the opportunity that the others had to land on the historic day gnawed at us. We understood, but we felt cheated.

Finally June 6th arrived. D-Day. Eisenhower had seized the eight- to ten-hour window of opportunity — a lull in the weather, a barely tolerable period of fair conditions. It was one of the last chances of the season to land the American Army on the shores of France. The place — St. Laurent-sur-Mer — code name, Omaha Beach. There were a number of harbors along the Normandy coast, but Hitler anticipated that Calais, the shortest distance between England and France, would be our choice. To throw him off, Eisenhower chose a stretch of coastline without ports or easy access, dominated by treacherous cliffs and raging surf. In the mean-time, General George S. Patton fumed in southeast England, faking activ-ity with a phantom army of rubber vehicles, mannequin paratroopers, and recorded tank noises.

The Normandy invasion had three prerequisites for its success: com-mand of the sea, command of the air, and dispersal of the German ground forces. Strategy and luck, planning and luck, secrecy and luck, and elabo-rate deception would be the deciding factors.

Six-hundred-thousand tons of concrete, 31,000 tons of steel, and 1.5 million yards of steel screening were used to construct the artificial har-bors, which included eight dry and two wet docks, known as "Mulberries." Over 70 old ships were sunk, and 146 concrete caissons, each called "Phoenix," were towed across the English Channel to form the break-waters known as "Gooseberries." Access to the shore, for the vehicles that had landed at the Mulberry docks, was provided by the "Whale" units — roadways across the waters. And oil pipelines, called "Pluto," each 70 miles long, were laid underwater. They would carry 120 million gallons of gasoline. The preparation of the artificial harbors alone required 3,000 craft and 15,000 men. Every piece of equipment was counted, down to the very last item — every piece except the coffins. Endless rows of burial boxes were stacked high in the corners of ships. With only 15 percent of the men having ever seen combat, no one knew when or how many coffins would be put to use.

All this activity was unknown to the Germans until D-Day because the Allies' complete air superiority prevented the enemy from sending recon-naissance aircraft. The year prior to D-Day had turned southern England into a military camp, and during the last three months, all civilian activity had ceased to exist within a ten-mile-wide strip of coastline. In addition, every piece of mail from England was curtailed, including the previously untouchable diplomatic pouches.

For the initial June 6th D-Day assault, over 287,000 men and 20,000 vehicles had to be loaded onto 4,200 LSTs and LCTs (Landing Ship Tanks and Landing Craft Tanks) supported by 1,200 merchant ships and 23 cruisers, and many destroyers. Upon the turbulent seas, the largest armada the world had ever known waited in readiness for the seemingly impossible set of circumstances to fall into place. If they didn't, the question would have to be asked, "What do we do with almost 300,000 men who have no place to go for the next two weeks?" Neither food nor shelter had been arranged for such a contingency. On land, in England, 3,000,000 troops were penned up in 1,108 Allied camps awaiting orders.

Time ticked on as every Normandy rock and wave was studied. Each man and machine had a specific place and a specific task. Because of submerged German mines, the landing had to take place just before dawn on a rising low tide. A full moon was preferable, but not mandatory. The target day, which depended on the weather, was termed "Y" day, June 1st. If that didn't work, then the next possible moment was Y+4, which penciled out to be June 5th, with the 6th or 7th still possible. After that, only the moonless June 19th was left. And the weather would have to be good, which was very unlikely. (As it happened, June 19th turned out to suffer the most violent Channel storm in recorded history, a storm that destroyed the breakwater at the Mulberry.)

When the order was finally given, Eisenhower launched the D-Day attack with the words:

> Good Luck! And let us all beseech the blessing of Almighty
> God upon this great and noble undertaking.

Then the pre-arranged poetic code ". . . *wounds my heart with a monotonous languor*" was broadcast to France, and the people knew the invasion had begun.

—◄○►—

The English Channel was an unforgiving mistress. With every cell in their bodies craving rest, the men waited, huddled in tight rolling quarters in ships and landing craft, illuminated by dim yellow light, retching from the stench of diesel oil and vomit. Finally the HMS *Belfast* fired the first broadside of the pre-invasion bombardment and in the next 24 hours American soldiers landed on the French shore at Omaha and Utah Beaches, in the American Sector. Simultaneously, the British and other Allies were going ashore at various beaches on our left flank. The anticipation and excitement were intoxicating. By the time the men left their floating metal craft to run out onto the open beach and face the unknown, they were exhausted and drained physically and emotionally.

At this point, for each man, it became *his* war. His initial goal was to find cover and then locate a way off the beach. But as ramps were lowered and the men charged into machine-gun fire, some were cut down by bullets or blown apart by mines; others drowned as they left their craft. Yet enough of them got through the initial assault to reach the sea wall above the beach, from where the entrenched Germans fired down on them. Those who made it fought their way through barbed wire zig-zagged along the sand, and four million mines and obstacles, all the while knowing that to stop was certain death. They pushed through the cries of agony and into explosions, debris, and the smell of sweat and feces expelled at the moment when life leaves the body — that moment of abrupt insult. Surrounded by the bloodied and mangled dead, one soldier praying on his knees was nudged to move on. He curled forward. He too was dead.

Spirits plummeted. But to survive, the trained and disciplined men had to insulate themselves from reality, a barrier that allowed them to sit amongst the fallen and eat their rations. Yet each man possessed a limit beyond which he could not be forced. As a soldier waited with the cold seeping into his body, loneliness, fear, and despair seeped into his soul. Every moment, every thought, became an avenue to destruction, if not physically, at least mentally. The threat of death traveled with every bullet seeking random targets.

Although not written for this moment, the words of Kipling's *Gunga Din* are a poignant statement of the invasion: ". . . he who sheds his blood with me shall be my brother." Many brothers were made that day.

◄o►

Meanwhile, still waiting in England, my code-breaking group, the first echelon of Detachment A, was eager to get into action. The time would soon come for us. We knew that the Allies had a foothold on the beaches. The air was filled with anticipation; adrenaline was pumping through our bodies, and the fever of excitement was everywhere. In the succeeding days, the early June weather, which was never good, turned worse. The Atlantic contorted into a tumultuous storm. Then, as it suddenly and surprisingly abated, we broke camp, knocking down tents and packing gear to become part of the long, slow-moving convoy heading to England's south coast.

In order to maintain a constant reception of German messages, we had to "leap frog" our advance. One of our echelon had to move forward and become operational before the next could temporarily stop operation for the move. It was now my echelon's turn to go. Major Turkel's diary reflects:

> The dawn came early and clearly. That is to say, we got up in pitch dark and stood stamping in a circle, cigarettes glowing. The tops of the great oaks in the meadows were lacy points against a lemon and rose yellow-gray band while all the rest of the world was misty blue gray. . . . The grass was bearded with silver, . . . every tight wrapped bud and little branch a gleaming candelabrum.

The countryside had become a giant military parking lot for the tools of war. As we inched toward Southampton, we passed through towns of wide-eyed children and adults lining the streets, watching and waving. Desperate hope peered from their eyes, a hungry longing for victory and peace. We were wide-eyed as well as we stared from our open trucks at field after field crammed with huge amounts of equipment: cannons, tanks, ammo, gasoline drums.

This 80-mile journey to the coast opened my eyes to the vastness of war and the complexity of the operation that filled this beautiful countryside. Upon arrival in Southampton we marched to the end of a pier, anticipating pick-up by a transport ship that would take us across the Channel. But just like our arrival in England, none awaited us. The diary of Operations Officer Lieutenant Mortimer Proctor of Detachment A states that his group, the second echelon, arrived and was directed to their "village" where the men received blankets, PX-rations for one week, and the first white bread since arriving in England. Following dinner he distributed partial pay — in *francs*.

The code word indicating that one was informed of the invasion was "bigot," so in the morning the second echelon was "bigoted," although this was somewhat after-the-fact, as it was the 30th of June. Following the briefing, Proctor's echelon proceeded to the "hard," the cement ramp that served as a dock for the LSTs. There he was shocked to find my echelon, which had left camp several days before him, still waiting. There was a good deal of ribbing about who was going to get to France first, and his group really rubbed it in. This bantering raised the spirits of his men but didn't do much for the first echelon who would spend the next three days in limbo. Proctor left a forlorn-looking group behind him on the dock. We were really ticked off. For the next three days we twiddled our thumbs and tried to contain our nervous energy, a very difficult feat for a bunch of young GIs ready for action.

Because we had been scheduled for immediate departure upon arrival at the docks, no food or shelter was available. This made us appreciate our previous C-rations, the tins of stews and soups and "stuff" that could be heated whenever we could find a fire. Now we were limited to the same old K-rations that we carried with us for the invasion, the boxes of bars — chocolate bars, cheese bars, dried fruit bars, all assorted flavors of cardboard — supplemented with Red Cross coffee and donuts. We searched out a piece of ground and vegetated in our foul-smelling, stiff, chemically impregnated clothing, using our helmets for seats and pillows.

Word spread that the ship that was to transport us had been torpedoed, so we watched as more and more troops arrived and departed for Normandy, leaving us stranded and frustrated. And when the buzz bombs started coming overhead 24 hours a day, the tension mounted. The V-1s were infernal little pilotless craft, much like miniature airplanes with short, stubby wings that created a putt-putting noise as they passed. When they ran out of fuel, there was an eerie moment of silence before they descended and exploded on a random target anywhere in southern England — a blast that could destroy a large building. This moment of silence was pure psychological warfare. It froze our guts. I would stop to look up, listen, and wait, expecting that each bomb was headed directly for me. Those moments left my nerves raw. Tension became unbearable and was heightened by both the whine and the anticipatory silence of the V-1s. Eight-thousand of these miserable little bombs were a product

of slave laborers forced to work in the 40 miles of tunnels and pas-
sageways comprising the largest underground factory in the world in
Germany.

Our previous excitement and anticipation by this time was tempered by
the sobering reports of the nearly inch-by-inch fighting in Normandy. Our
hopes for a quick breakthrough and a mad dash to the German frontier
were crushed. And so was our envy for those who had gone before us, as
reports filtered back across the Channel of the lives that had been lost. The
Unit History of Detachment B reports:

> [We] had no way of knowing what had happened to those
> who had left . . . weeks ago, and the news of . . . death came as
> a surprise as the nature of our work gave everyone a feeling of
> comparative safety. Some of the men were even more anxious
> to get over there now, but others began wishing the date for a
> sailing would be postponed.

I was beginning to see my place in the war, and the words of World War
I poet Gilbert Franhau became reality:

> I am only a cog in a giant machine, a
> link of an endless chain: —
>   And the rounds are drawn, and the rounds
>   are fired, and the empties return again. . . .

While we waited at the Southampton dock, a variety of craft took men
and transports across the Channel. Some were the LCTs — nothing more
than small seagoing tank carriers — like a large open rowboat with an
enclosed area for the coxswain or skipper; and others were the huge 300-
foot LSTs that could, like the LCT, lower their six-foot end wall into the
sand, making a loading and unloading ramp for men and vehicles.

Lieutenant Proctor was lucky enough to cross the Channel on a ship
with luxurious quarters and fondly remembers his passage in the finest bed
he had slept in in months:

> The room was air-conditioned [and had] an Austrian shower
> which worked. The ward room was very comfortable with
> leather furniture, magazines and books, and a kitchenette . . . in

which coffee was always available [and] an ice box with . . . the
materials for making sandwiches.

Vehicles that were being transported on the LSTs, along with the
men, had to be driven up a steep ramp to the lower deck, the tank deck,
and from there an elevator took them to the top deck where the drivers
squeezed them in between ventilators and hoists and chained them
down for the duration. Some drivers were told to move their vehicles onto
large nets that were then pulled skyward by gigantic cranes, rocking
precariously over the decks and the men before being lowered into the
LST's hold. Soldiers from Detachment B scurried like fleeing rats when
one of the ammo-laden trucks came crashing through the deck after
slipping from its rigging. You didn't have to wait for Jerry to be endan-
gered.

Each detachment of 3rd Radio Squadron Mobile was scheduled to land
in Normandy at a different time. Corporal Albert Gruber of Detachment B
had left Bristol on June 1st with the intention of putting ashore after the
initial thrust on the evening of D-Day. But the whole landing operation got
fouled up. For three days his boat kept circling to avoid becoming a target.
Finally, it anchored not far from the cruiser USS *Augusta*, which was
engaged in firing salvos toward shore. He recalls that the *Augusta* had
large six- or eight-inch guns, and your clothes would ripple from the con-
cussion. To break the boredom, the men counted the seconds between the
flash of the guns and the sound of the explosion and guessed the distance
to the target. It was a lot like what we did as children when trying to
figure out how far apart thunder and lightning were, but this time so
much more was at stake. Geysers resulting from the enemy artillery sent a
cold shower of sea water over the unprotected men, soaking them to the
skin.

My echelon hurriedly boarded an LST that had unexpectedly appeared
alongside the Southampton dock, as twilight turned into darkness. After
having sat on the pier for days under the buzz bombs I was frustrated, cold,
hungry, and scared. By the time I actually boarded the ship, my usually
observant mind was blank. Perhaps I slept. Perhaps I numbed myself to
the looming danger. Maybe it was the metal walls of the craft that shut out
the world, or I was simply too exhausted to care. But for me it is forgotten history. Perhaps this is why I was later surprised to learn that I had
crossed the Channel in the same transport, and climbed down the same

rope net into a small landing craft with another soldier, and yet never met him. The man was Lieutenant Peter White who was traveling with Detachment A at the time to join B. He had originally been assigned to A, but because he had studied in Germany in the early '30s and spoke excellent German, Captain Silverstein decided that he needed White to run Detachment B's Operations Room. This led him to become known as the "Scrounger."

An additional surprise was to find that there had been a heated exchange on the landing craft between Lieutenant White and my Commanding Officer, Captain Brinson. When White was boarding the boat, he had a camera around his neck. Brinson growled, "You can't take that with you." White replied, "I know. I'm putting it away." Brinson exploded. In front of all the men, he severely dressed down White, something that is just not done in the presence of enlisted men. To this day, White vividly remembers his embarrassment and his anger.

Our LST had anchored offshore around midnight and nervously awaited the dawn, floating on a relatively calm sea. Those before us had arrived in a churning ocean and a gagging stink of bile. The ones who had avoided seasickness during the crossing finally succumbed to the overwhelming smell of its victims. Vomit was everywhere as the men were tossed around like apples bobbing in a tub. Their bodies and minds had been stretched to the limit. And now it was just beginning, as we waited for our smaller craft to take us ashore.

———————◄○►———————

It was three weeks after D-Day, and now my turn to land. I stood at the side of the huge LST, lost in thought, wondering what the day would bring. The sway of the craft mesmerized me into a false calm as I peered into the inky blackness.

Suddenly the entire horizon erupted in a clamorous, multicolored display of cannon fire. A handful of German bombers tried to weave their way over our lines in order to drop their loads into the ship-crowded waters. The abruptness of the explosion made us dive for cover, but our mouths dropped open by the unexpected display before us — a sight so spectacular that our first moment of fright was dissolved by fascination. Although it lasted only a few minutes, it was the most impressive fireworks display I was to see in my lifetime. As the racket subsided, a slow Dixie drawl commented, "Does seem a mite uhly fo' the fo'th of Joolah." It was July 1. From then on I learned to live with constant noise — the thunder of guns, the roar of trucks, the rumble of tanks. It never stopped.

As the sun slowly rose, I had my first view of the Daliesque beachhead in full sun. I was aghast. We were surrounded by funnels and masts of sunken ships. A hush of apprehension fell as we began viewing the devastation and chaos. Fear gnawed at our guts. We wondered what catastrophe had taken place, and into what we were heading. Later I learned about the "Gooseberries," the artificially made breakwaters created by sunken ships, but at the time, thinking the Germans were responsible for all the destruction, my earlier bravado had paled. Fortunately, my uneasiness was tempered by an eagerness to meet the unknown and a youthful belief in immortality.

In order to board the bobbing LCT that would take us ashore from the larger craft, we descended the rope cargo nets, hand-over-hand. When my turn came, I jumped from the net at the same moment that a soldier above dropped his M-1 carbine directly onto my helmet. Stunned, I landed half in and half out of the waiting boat. Quick hands pulled me onto the deck before my body was crushed between the two rolling craft. At the time, I was reeling from the jolt, but I'll never forget that clumsy guy. He had a very young, smooth, scrubbed-looking face, the kind that always looks like it has just come from a shower, and prematurely gray hair. He was completely ill-equipped to be a soldier. If he had followed orders, the accident would never have happened. Under his jacket he had smuggled his radio, and when it came time to transfer from one boat to the next he was unable to hold on to both radio and carbine, so I got the brunt of his screwup. It was fortunate that I never saw him again because I might have laid him out cold. There were always some like him in the military — uncommitted and undisciplined. These "sad sacks" made the war more dangerous because you could never prepare for their incompetence.

Relieved that I had escaped the casualty list, I learned later that Corporal Richard Soderholm of Detachment B had not been as fortunate. Before embarkation at the marshaling area in England, all equipment had to be waterproofed as much as possible by taping closed gas masks and fitting rubber hoses into the exhaust pipes of vehicles so that the hoses stuck up above the windshield. Every spark plug, wire, and distributor ignition coil had to be covered with caulking. Six-foot ventilator tubes were attached to fuel tanks, radiators, engines, and carburetors. Each vehicle was then driven into a water-filled ditch to be tested. It was a necessary and tedious process. At the time of the crossing, some of the soldiers even covered the muzzle of their rifle with a condom, knowing that a steady supply certainly would be forthcoming.

After Soderholm and the first echelon of Detachment B landed in Normandy, the unit regrouped and started up the heights towards Cricqueville, nothing more than an intersection of narrow dirt roads in the middle of endless fields. Corporal Al Gruber, who had been in one of the operating vans, remembers:

> We heard the gas alarm, so everybody got out their gas mask
> . . . [and] we were yelling, "Take off the tape. Take off the tape."
> Soderholm was sitting on a camouflage net in the corner of the
> van and . . . apparently didn't take the tape off. . . . He wasn't
> . . . saying anything or moving and when the all clear came . . .
> one of the fellows took it off and found that he was all blue in
> the face. We thought he had suffocated.

Never expecting a fatality in a non-combat unit, it was doubly difficult for Lieutenant Jim Copp to write the dreaded letter home informing Soderholm's mother of her son's death — a painful job which fell to the commissioned officers. Before putting pen to paper he went through the Corporal's belongings and found several chemically impregnated uniforms and gas masks in his gear, although only one set had been issued to each man. It was ironic that Soderholm's terror of a gas attack had led to his fatal reaction. Official military records show that he died from sniper fire, but the actual cause of death was suffocation. It was the only fatality that occurred in our unit.

In May of 1997 I visited his grave in France. With a cloudless, silent sky above and the wind whipping about, emotion washed over me. I recalled a stanza of Rupert Brooke's poem "The Dead":

> These laid the world away; poured out the red
> Sweet wine of youth; gave up the years to be
> Of work and joy, and that unhoped serene,
> That men call age; and those who would have been,
> Their sons, they gave, their immortality.

Other soldier's graves have been visited by American tourists since the end of the war and one cemetery has a guest book to record the people and their thoughts. Thousands of names appear on the ledger alongside: "Son," "Wife," "Friend." A particularly poignant entry shows the name of a French couple and the single word, *"Merci."*

————◄o►————

Corporal Soderholm's Commander, Lieutenant Fred Gottlieb, of the first echelon of Detachment B, recalls the many anxious seasick days circling offshore in his LST after sailing from Bristol on the 1st of June. He had expected to land on June 6th. The command had fallen to him rather than Heinrich because he was single. His orders were to hit the beach, proceed to a designated location, set up their 100-foot antenna, and begin logging traffic as soon as possible. But contrary to the beach master's signal, the Navy Lieutenant in charge gave a premature order to lower the ramp and disembark. It turned into a fiasco. Even though there were only 8 vehicles and 40 personnel in the echelon, it took 12 hours to complete disembarkation. Almost everything that could go wrong did.

Lieutenant Gottlieb was concerned as his lead vehicle drove off the ramp and struck a sand bank. This was a heavily mined area. After a moment, however, he realized that all was well and attempted to proceed to shore, but water had gotten into the engine and it stalled. The driver gunned it, flooded it, and cursed it. Nothing happened. The men sat unprotected in the back of the truck as sniper fire starting coming off the cliffs. "Stop fooling with it. You're becoming a German target," yelled the barge Commander.

Gottlieb was one of the last in his group to land. Suddenly his truck began to sink. Not knowing just how deep the water was, he told his men to discard everything and swim for it. Corporal Al Gruber remembers someone yelling, "Choke it, choke it." What was meant was to cover the ventilator hoses so that water couldn't get in, not to choke the engine, but in the heat of the moment this only added to the confusion. Staff Sergeant Robert Siefert's memoirs record the incident:

> Since the truck I was driving was one of the next two in line,
> it was my turn to go first. Everyone was cautioning the drivers
> to go slow and take it easy, not to get excited. The instant I felt

the front wheels hit the sand I poured the gas to it and parted the water til I hit high ground. As we traveled to higher ground there we saw destruction that cannot be described, tanks and half tracks sitting with the tracks blown off, dead bodies floating in the water. One man rescuing the bodies picked up a piece of a leg with a boot on it and waved at us.

Gruber adds:

> [The Navy guy] left us hanging in the water. . . . [It] was probably up to the wheels at that time. So we sat there, probably 200 yards from shore. The tide washing in and we were waiting for someone to come along and pick us up off this truck. Our duffel bags are in the back of the six by six and we're sitting there in seats and the water's coming up. . . . It came up almost underneath the benches. Our duffel bags were all wet, our legs were all wet.

Within an hour Gruber's vehicle was completely submerged by the fast incoming tide. Government records show that two amphibious vehicles took Gottlieb and 20 men off his truck, and then the LST proceeded to an adjoining beach and unloaded the remaining vehicles; but Gottlieb remembers swimming to shore. Not knowing that it was the American Navy officer and not the British beach master who had given the premature landing order, he shook his fist in the air and charged. In a dripping wet fury, he screamed in his thick, Berlin accent, "How could you do such a stupid thing. You're supposed to be trained." The beach master, not happy with such treatment, drew his pistol and yelled, "Get the hell out of here."

At this point Gottlieb realized that he was out of line and withdrew just as sniper fire started coming in. His party dove for cover behind what was later discovered to be live ammunition boxes. When they were able to regroup, they loaded into their trucks and started up the incline, only to be startled by the sound of a gas alarm — the false alarm that led to Soderholm's death.

Approximately a week later, the second echelon of Detachment B, under Captain Silverstein and Lieutenant Copp, was still waiting at their English port for their long overdue orders. All they could do was try to amuse themselves and listen to the battle that was going on across the Channel. When orders finally came for them to be sent to Utah Beach instead of Omaha Beach, they were livid. B was supposed to connect with Gottlieb, who was setting up an antenna to log enemy traffic and pass information on to advance headquarters. Failure to link up with B's first echelon meant that secret information in Captain Silverstein's possession could not be used, thereby severely limiting the function of Lieutenant Gottlieb's unit.

Silverstein recalls that the landing at Utah on June 15th, several days late, caused a great deal of difficulty in reaching their ultimate target, Omaha, because it put them on the other side of the Merderet River. Logistically this created a mess. Fortunately his men were well disciplined — unlike an infantry unit that had landed upstream and tried to get across the river in a rubber boat. One of the men, saturated with Calvados, began singing, "Row, row, row your boat," at the top of his lungs. The sky exploded with German artillery rounds, resulting in heavy casualties. According to Copp, "This was just the beginning of a series of fiascoes."

Upon landing, an MP sent Detachment B toward Cherbourg, the opposite direction from their destination. As they moved along, the landscape became littered with the dead — Americans, Germans, livestock. Cows, with their legs awkwardly askew and bloated from the gas of death, lay beside humans rotting in the rain. Sounds of battle increased and Army trucks returning with dead soldiers became more and more frequent. Everyone was stunned. When they realized that they were going the wrong way, the world seemed to turn upside-down. With great difficulty and frustration they eventually got proper directions and turned themselves around in the choked mass of decay. But because of the congestion, they couldn't get through and had to spend the night enveloped in the smell of death in soggy terrain that had been deliberately flooded by the Germans. Many of the men were forced to sleep in water-filled foxholes during a torrential downpour. Lieutenant Copp remembers:

> It was a terrible night. I slept under a two-and-a-half ton truck for protection and listened to the nearby battle all night as power shifted between the Americans and the Germans. Our little convoy had had to go through enemy territory and "fluid" territory (belonging to no one) to get to Omaha. Everything was dead; Jerries, G.I.'s, cows with their legs sticking skyward . . .

broken gliders with the black and white insignias of the Allies. We passed through a vast wasteland where a plane was coming straight at us and we were terrified. For some unknown reason there was a machine gun mounted on our mess truck and the cooks decided to go against orders and shoot down the plane. Not knowing what they were doing, they were unsuccessful and watched the plane come closer and closer. Just before it hit the ground we recognized it as one of our own fighters crashing to earth, not the enemy on a suicide mission.

——◄○►——

Our landing — Detachment A — had been relatively easy, and we crossed the beach without incident. The jeeps labored up the steep path to the top of the cliff and a battered blue and white signpost reading "Colleville." We had been assigned to Cricqueville-en-Bessin, a few kilometers to the south, where the efficient MPs quickly helped us find the way to our campsite about five miles from the front. The countryside turned to six-inch-deep mud as the sunny morning changed to pouring rain for our unloading.

Under a natural camouflage of apple trees we set up the radios and antennae and immediately ran into a number of technical problems. There had been no prior consultation regarding the feasibility of reception from this location, and heavy interference on the cross-Channel frequencies plagued us, requiring a lot of experimenting with our antennae. Tanks and trucks moving along the narrow roads repeatedly cut our lines, and the unpredictable British vehicles and equipment that had proven so troublesome in Chalfont St. Giles continued to thwart us here, particularly the temperamental machines that required frequent adjustments. In addition, the Germans changed their encoding procedure, thereby causing a great deal of difficulty for the Intelligence department. This significantly slowed down our decoding, until we were able to figure out their new method.

During this arduous time Captain Brinson wandered through our little cubbyhole checking on us and our work. One of the men mentioned that there was a lot of "QRM" (static). Brinson's response was typically bewildering. "Great," he said, "keep up the good work." And he wandered out the door. It felt just like our overseas physical exam.

At noon on July 4th our front-line artillery reminded us of home by setting off a tremendous eruption of ammunition. By July 6th we had established courier service among all detachments, 9th Air Force Head-quarters, and the British Air Ministry. Five days later, all the telephone and teletype lines were laid, making us fully operational and providing a complete squadron network. The land line between Detachments A and B was particularly useful since it enabled us to fix the position of German aircraft with considerable accuracy.

While we were working on the technical problems, Lieutenant Proctor was working on getting us fed. Each unit had to arrange to draw its own rations, get water, and dispose of garbage. This should have been easy and routine, except that everything had to be processed through a Lieutenant at "Gangway" — 9th Air Force HQ — a little man who enjoyed exerting his enormous power. Acting as if he was paying for everything himself, and treating us as if we were asking for a handout, he forced Proctor to beg and cajole for our food.

It was frequently difficult to concentrate on our work because many messages came through accompanied by the heavy static that apparently bothered us more than it did Captain Brinson, but we much preferred the excitement of work to the boredom of inactivity.

As soon as 3rd RSM became operational, the radio came alive with the excited voice of a German pilot, *"Periskop auf. Periskop auf."* Instantly the men were on alert. *Periscope up*? It didn't make sense. Pilots had their own codes, their own jargon as they talked to one another, but this time our voice interceptors couldn't determine what code they were using. Jerry had been sending "spoof" messages designed to fool us. Was this one of those? Or was it simply the height of frivolity that they sometimes engaged in to convey nothing more serious than a special greeting? These nonsense messages were usually prefaced with the individual code of the operator. The ELGAR code that we in Detachment A constantly worked with was part of a group of codes named for musical composers and was understood to convey German messages for their anti-aircraft units — the "curtain of steel" for our aircraft over Germany. Now, however, there was what appeared to be a nonsense message, and not proceeded by a call sign.

The Direction Finders got a fix on the German planes and the puzzle became more confusing. The aircraft were far inland, nowhere near any submarines. What could *"Periscope up! Periscope up!"* possibly mean? We scurried around trying to figure it out, but finally admitted defeat. We were completely baffled. It wasn't until after the war that we learned the meaning behind the strange message.

As one of the "new" boys in the outfit I was ordered to dig the officers latrine. In my required stiff woolen uniform that sealed me into its airtight cocoon, I soon found myself sweating profusely in the stifling heat and questioning my "Intelligence" duties. My skin couldn't breathe, and I became completely soaked. Just as I reached half the required depth, an air-raid alarm sounded and two officers dashed headlong into MY latrine. Without stopping to salute, I jumped out and left the rest of the digging to the next soldier on duty.

After the latrines came the foxholes, with locations allocated according to rank. "Old timers" got the protecting hedgerows. The rest of us got the open fields, exposed to the elements and possible enemy fire.

Normandy, a damp fertile farm country, provided easy digging but lousy sleeping. With the constant flashing in the night sky and artillery roaring overhead, it was difficult to relax. The GIs on guard duty would shoot up the bushes for no other reason than sheer panic. The amount of shrapnel discharged convinced us that the officers were not overreacting when they ordered us to wear our helmets at all times. After a week in my chilly moist hole I developed a bladder problem that prevented me from getting to the latrine. Using my versatile helmet as a urinal, I threw the contents up over the edge, always checking wind direction first. On sunny days the smell of the warm, steamy urine-saturated soil surrounding the foxhole made life miserable for my foxhole buddy, Len Rosenberg. He became very motivated to improve the situation and miraculously found some creosote to sprinkle on the ground. The odor of the waterproofing chemical was just as pungent, but not as offensive. I was grateful. The creosote helped both my nose and my bladder condition. I had learned that my helmet could be handy in a variety of situations: pillow, washbowl, barf bowl, cooking pot, and urinal.

By this time the constant din of roaring, rumbling, and ack ack began to become an unconscious part of my life, no more noticeable than the distant thunder of a summer storm in Queens. If my mind and body had been unable to shut out the intrusions, I would not have survived emotionally.

Although we had no mess tent and were forced to eat in the open, we did have a field kitchen. Some of the units had the pleasure of music floating continuously from tree-mounted loudspeakers as they sat in the bee-infested apple orchard or back in their foxholes. All of us loved the wonderful cider made from the overhanging fruit — a welcome substitute for the horrible halazone-flavored water. Using cigarettes, some of us bartered for five-gallon containers of the beverage along with homemade cheese and bread and an occasional chicken that we boiled in a helmet.

For the first few weeks in France I had only a distant church steeple for orientation in the endless landscape. Every field was jammed with troops or equipment as more and more men arrived daily. Because of the increasing size of our unit, the apple orchard no longer provided adequate camouflage, so flat tops and nets were used to hide installations.

A temporary fighter landing strip constructed with perforated steel plates — PSP — was built next to our encampment at Cricqueville, the first in France, for P-51 Mustangs of the famous 354th Fighter Group. Around its perimeter were quadruple-mounted machine guns for anti-aircraft defense. As soon as it was finished, the Mustangs arrived. They came in so low it seemed that they were landing right next to me.

One day, we had an unexpected visitor. In shock, we watched as a German plane approached the landing strip and began its descent. No one could believe what was happening. With wide eyes and dropped jaws, we watched in broad daylight as the plane touched down, taxied to the end of the runway, turned around and took off again. I'm sure that the German pilot was just as startled as we were, and I hope that he survived the war to tell his grandchildren about the biggest "whoops" in his flying career. Fortunately for him, the gunners manned their stations only at night. Today, whenever I see a touchdown run in the wrong direction, I'm reminded of that pilot.

————◄o►————

Under the direction of Sergeant Boyd, some of our men were able to wangle a couple of auxiliary fuel tanks from the planes and, with faucets and a nozzle from a wrecked ship, erect a makeshift shower. From a wooden scaffold that held the tanks, canvas was hung around the frame for a bit of privacy, making it look more like today's rocket launch pad than a temporary bathroom — but it worked beautifully. We had hot and cold running water tanks under which each of us was allowed to spend two strictly timed minutes. It was really delicious, and it wasn't until we were clean again that we realized just how smelly we had become. I had been as ripe as Limburger cheese. We also had the luxury of a paperless and quite public outdoor latrine that consisted of nothing more than a raised board placed over a deep hole in the ground.

We finally got the camp in order and our equipment working and settled into a daily routine. Unfortunately Lieutenant Copp had brought some luxury items from home that really irritated his fellow officers:

> I had an electric razor which you know, at that time nobody had, and I'd plug it in to shave. "Stop that. Stop that. We're listening to the radio."

Not only was the noise itself a nuisance, but every time he plugged it in, it blew a circuit. "What am I going to do? I have to shave," he complained. To stop him from blowing fuses, his men had the maintenance department jerry-rig a bunch of batteries that they got from Lieutenant White's collection of scrounged paraphernalia procured from his many sorties in Normandy.

It was at this time, one very hot afternoon, that a GI dashed out of the command tent and began beating a metal triangle, like a mad cook summoning ranch hands to dinner. This was the prearranged signal for a gas attack. Immediately everyone followed the systematic procedure:

1. Drop to one knee.
2. Put on the gas mask.
3. Unroll the regulation gas cape required to be carried on your belt at all times and pull it over your head and body.
4. Wait for the all clear.

As I languished in the stifling July heat, I felt the sweat trickle down my face. My uniform became soaked, the air diminished, and I thought I was going to suffocate. Which kind of death would be worse, gas or asphyxiation? I wondered. It was masochism *à la mode*. At what seemed to be my very last breath, the all clear sounded and the loudspeakers announced that it was only smoke, not gas. The Germans had been shelling the front all day, and in the late afternoon they hit one of their own ammunition dumps, sending great clouds of smoke and dust into the air. Mistaking the haze for gas, a jeep-load of panicky soldiers came roaring through camp yelling, "This is it! This is it! This is it!" Either to escape the smoke or believing that this was gas, the surrounding GIs had put on gas masks, and the rumor quickly spread. The false alarm paralyzed the American sector for 20 minutes, and word had it that someone was going to be court-martialed. We never found out if that happened.

Not being a combat unit, casualties came to the members of Detachment A as a surprise. One day I heard a small, unidentifiable popping sound, and later discovered that one of the guys had found an empty German artillery shell and decided to hammer it into an ashtray. When it blew up in his hand, it took off three fingers. The official military document recorded the incident as, "The Detachment suffered its first casualty on July 16th. Corporal Dan E. O'Brien was accidentally injured when a German shell exploded while he was attempting to remove the charge." For this he was awarded the Purple Heart.

We had one other non-battle casualty when Corporal Worth was wounded by a fragment from a 500-pound bomb that was detonated by a bomb disposal squad. This was another enemy-from-within episode, as the Army had failed to station guards and warning signs in the area alerting soldiers of the danger.

Several nights later we became directly involved in battle, the first of only a few times in the entire war. It was a surprise because we didn't expect to be exposed to danger. Jerry had been flying over our camp every night, right on schedule, but he always ignored us on his way elsewhere. We knew that we weren't his target so we had grown complacent about the roar of his planes. We merely listened and watched, but never felt threatened. This night was different. At about 1:30 a.m., Corporal Al Gruber was on radio intercept duty and picked up, "My bombs are on target." As the Direction Finders were trying to locate the source of the transmission, the air around us suddenly exploded with the sound of guns. Scattered German bombers were heading for the beach unloading area. We suddenly realized that we were listening to German pilots talking about their raid on us! This bizarre experience was "real time" Intelligence, something that had never happened to us before. The Germans were bombing directly over our heads at the same time that we were receiving their transmissions!

The Duty officer, Hugh Davidson, had just settled down in the Intelligence caravan for his first night on a luxurious cot, rather than the vehicle's usual hard floor. He found himself sitting in the middle of the caravan covered with sand. The British had used the truck in the Egyptian desert before requisitioning it for European service and the force of the explosions had shaken it so hard that sand sifted from every crevice. Other officers ran from their tents and congregated in a ditch in the hedgerow to protect themselves from possible further action. This congenial crowd sitting in pajamas and helmets looked like schoolboys at a come-as-you-are slumber party waiting to be cast in some B movie. Because our unit was not supposed to be subjected to combat, it was a shock to find ourselves under fire. Not much damage occurred, except to our radio van, our nerves, and me.

As one of the German planes descended in our direction with its tail in flames, the pilot released his load. Fascinated by the descending mines, each attached to a parachute, I crouched in my foxhole watching them fall to earth. The explosion hit full force, and I was thrown to the ground by the pressure wave. *My God, the enemy is trying to kill ME!*

Feeling as if an elephant was standing on my back, I realized for the first time that this was serious stuff — stuff I didn't like. Dazed and gasping, I struggled to my feet, and like a fool, poked my head out of the hole to watch the plane, now completely ablaze, crash into the sea. A moment later a fragment from one of our anti-aircraft artillery shells lodged in my left eye. I felt more chagrined than scared for having been so stupid as to have stuck my head up. The night wore on and I became increasingly uncomfortable as the piece of metal seemed to grow larger and the pain intensified.

The following morning, the top Sergeant gave me permission to go to the nearest field hospital a half-mile away where I got into the long line of "walking wounded." As the line wove its way through stretchers of moaning, bloodied men, I couldn't help compare the scene to a Goya sketch. Without any visible injury, I felt quite sheepish and out of place and would have gladly bolted back to my unit if the pain in my eye had not become so unbearable. Finally, the medic who was sitting on an empty ammunition crate examined me. He took out two Q-tips, rolled back my eyelid, and quickly picked out the piece of metal. The injury was a good lesson.

Jerry flew over our camp every night, sometimes just to cause chaos and disruption, but I was no longer as curious. I had had my wartime injury, and it was an experience I didn't relish repeating. Our own AA fire caused more damage to 3rd RSM than the enemy bombs, and the flak whizzing through the trees every night left our nerves jagged. Lieutenant Proctor's diary, however, adds his very poetic perspective:

> Nothing in war is more beautiful than the red streams of tracer fire — it rising slowly in a great arc, each bullet going at an apparently very leisure speed . . . a lovely sight.

It certainly was, but I wasn't going to look any more.

The Unit History of Detachment B records:

> On July 29 at 0130 hours, we had one of the most exciting nights in the detachment's existence. A group of German planes came over our area, apparently heading towards the sea. Our anti-aircraft opened up into the darkness on the planes and although the sky was cloudy one of the attackers was hit. In a short while, through the light of gunfire, several small objects were seen floating down over a field adjacent to ours. A sudden explosion, and the operations vehicles parked by the hedges rocked on their wheels. The two guards standing at the gate when the explosion came plunged headlong, burying their heads into the "good earth." . . . Some of our men were thrown from their beds to the ground. A radio van in the next field [Detachment A's] had been hit and the transmitter caught fire, lighting up the entire sky. Over in the Motor Pool . . . Cpl. Strobeck was sleeping. That night he had had a few drinks and then had gone to sleep naked. The concussions were so great that the ropes on his tent snapped. The Cpl. jumped up and threw his nude body into the nearest briar and bramble filled ditch. . . . The men wakened suddenly to find only their square of six cots standing in the open, their tent blown halfway into the next area. . . .

After the bombing, many of the men started digging their foxholes deeper, some in such a frenzy that John O'Hara, one of our crack radio operators, speculated that they certainly might wind up in China.

These July 1944 days were frequently uneventful, but one morning the drone of aircraft increased and the curdled-cloud heavens quickly filled with the black silhouettes of Allied bombers sweeping across the morning sky. The roar of the engines pulled my eyes upward to watch as the aircraft flew overhead in tight formation, moving as one giant dark mass. It seemed that the sky had become an ocean as ships — aircraft — in wave after wave passed.

Excitement filled the camp. I watched the planes and felt more than four million pounds of bombs explode along the U.S. front. The words of Homer came to mind: "Our arrows darken the sun. Our chariots make the earth tremble." My earth was certainly trembling, and this sudden action meant only one thing — our soldiers were breaking through and were on their way down the Normandy peninsula, fanning out across Brittany and moving toward Paris. Soon we would follow.

It was a thrilling realization. The infantry's purpose had been to cut through and surround the Germans, but they had been unable to do so. When the invasion began, we had expected it to be quick and easy. It was now almost two months later and what was to have been a passing-through point, Normandy, was crammed with men and equipment bottled up in a space that was decreasing rapidly. For awhile it felt like a balloon ready to burst. Finally, it did, and the breakthrough began.

Shortly after establishing camp I was sent back to Omaha Beach on an errand. As I made my way down the escarpment to the sand, I took in the panorama of destruction before me. Some of the men in the LSTs had misjudged the depth of the water and the ramps had been lowered prematurely. Many soldiers on those craft had rushed forward with full packs, and finding no foothold, sank to their death. Others had died in the tanks.

Cranes were at work hauling the sunken vehicles of D-Day out of the water. The Army had "dressed" Sherman tanks in inflatable rubber, theorizing that they would be made floatable by the "skirts" and would therefore drive through the surf to the sand and shield the infantry. This would have been possible in a glass-calm sea, but the surf on June 6th had been wrought by the slashing fire of the German guns as they shredded the "skirts," sending the tanks and crews under.

Death was everywhere. Engineers pulled bodies out of open hatches — one came apart in a soldier's hands. By a serious flaw in the timetable, some soft-skinned vehicles had arrived too early and found themselves in the middle of battle, only to be torn apart by German bullets. Meanwhile, brave men struggled to form a human chain to help non-swimmers make it to shore. Most didn't.

The horror of the beach shot a shiver through my heart. The uniform of one unfortunate soldier was jammed in the tracks of a tank, hopefully run over after he had died. I was grateful that it was not me. My tears flowed as I struggled to accept the insanity and faced my mortality.

◄○►

As the war progressed and Detachment A's work became more strategic in nature, we found ourselves becoming increasingly more associated with SHAEF than 9th Air Force.

Chapter Seven

Movin' Out

HE ORIGINAL DETACHMENTS comprising 3rd RSM — Able, Baker, and Charlie — came together for the one and only time in Normandy. Before leaving Criqueville, a cadre of six men from Flap B was taken back to England by Lieutenant Fred Gottlieb to begin forming D. Flap C, under Lieutenant Kurt Heinrich, waited in France for General Patton's Third Army to fill out its ranks with new men flown directly from the States by order of Major Turkel's powerful "Lusty Letter," giving him the right to ask for anything or anyone for any reason.

In August of 1944 Detachment D recorded:

> The new detachment [D], numbering approximately 80 men, was made up of an "Old Timers" Group who had

been with Headquarters Detachment . . . and a larger new group who had just arrived from the States. The new D Detachment then met its Commanding Officer, 1st Lt. Ferdinand Gottlieb who had come from B Detachment.

From Normandy, Detachments A, B, and C fanned out in different directions in a general south and southeasterly course, moving eventually toward Paris — sometimes occupying the same territory, but never at the same time. As our movements became more fluid, there was some tongue-in-cheek discussion about changing the name from 3rd Radio Squadron (Mobile) to 3rd Radio Squadron (*Volatile*).

The squadron's fifth detachment, Flap Easy, Detachment E, was seldom mentioned, and very little is known about it except for Lieutenant Peter White's recollections:

> Detachment E? I can tell you about E. E was the communications detachment, and it never was part of the squadron in the sense that it was never where anybody could see them. They were the ones who were supposed to make sure that the people back in England were getting our reports.

The Unit History of E states that it was "the funneling unit for intelligence information for the squadron." E was a very integral part of the operation, but had no real interaction with us. The TOP SECRET report, *United States Cryptologic History, American Signal Intelligence in Northwest Africa and Western Europe*, prepared in 1980 by George F. Howe for the National Security Agency, states:

> . . . Detachment "E" was primarily used for communications, for the exchange of information among the detachments, and for passing along information obtained from broadcasts from England. . . . During the latter part of the Battle of the Bulge [it] was to be of particular value, enhanced by the failure of land-lines. . . .

As the war progressed and Detachment A's work became more strategic in nature, we found ourselves becoming increasingly more associated with SHAEF than 9th Air Force. Detachment A developed a certain éclat, and became an entity unto itself. As we moved, we were kept farther from the front than the other detachments, leading me to believe that we were "special" because of our work and the important strategic information that we had in our possession. Later I realized that it was probably because of our closer relationship with SHAEF and also because B, C, and D's radio/telephone receivers had shorter range and had to move closer for reception!

While we were stuck in Normandy I took every opportunity to see the countryside. Hitching a ride into the famous town of Bayeux in the English sector of the front, I found only two small shops on the main street still open. Although goods were extremely scarce and their shelves almost bare, I found a few delicacies. The first shop was a *laiterie* — a dairy shop — where I bought a small wheel of freshly made Brie with the owner's admonition that I must wait a few days before eating, to allow it to ripen. After living on K-rations for several weeks, it was difficult to follow his advice, but I tucked it under my arm and went into the adjacent store, which sold lingerie embroidered with Alençon lace. The only items of interest were the brassieres. Nonchalantly the clerk displayed her wares before me, and too embarrassed to handle them, I visually made my decision and pointed. My mother was to be the recipient. Years later I was to find out that one size does *not* fit all. With a twinkle in her eye, she told me how she had unwrapped it with much amusement. I had sent a beautiful lace bra made to fit an under-developed teenage girl!

Lieutenant Peter White also bought some Alençon lace and sent it home to his wife. Over 50 years later it is still being kept for a special occasion. I never knew what happened to my lace bra, but I've often wondered how much war lace is being stored in cedar chests around the country.

I returned to camp with my treasured Brie and brassiere. Digging a little shelf in my foxhole to store the cheese, I ignored the barbs around me complaining of the stink. Although it looked ripe enough, I still refused to eat it until it was ready — a decision I've always regretted. One more day passed, and it was time to indulge, but to my chagrin, the Brie had disappeared. Everyone piously denied knowing anything, convincing me that someone had thrown it away.

Lieutenant Proctor had the good fortune of visiting Bayeux when there was more abundance, and all sorts of surprising things were for sale that were unavailable elsewhere — souvenirs, furniture, china, food. Because Bayeux was the only large town in liberated France that was not off-limits, it was filled with soldiers and Brits. The only negative to his visit was the dense white dust on the heavily traveled roads surrounding the town that he said got into your mouth, ears, eyes and clothes and seemed to stay there. This dust contained a hard silicon-like material that played havoc with aircraft engines. Clouds of dust hung everywhere as tanks, trucks, and combat boots moved across Europe, chewing up the roads.

It seemed as if we were either plagued with dust or mud. Turkel observed:

> When an army is through with a piece of land, all that is left is elevation and distance . . . just the trucks going back and forth across the face of the land can chop and churn the whole surface until nothing is left but plops and clods and soupy masses of mud.

Lieutenant Proctor was overwhelmed with the beauty of the countryside contrasted with the increasing destruction he encountered:

> The country from here [Cricqueville] to St. Lo is perhaps more beautiful than even the best parts of England.

But upon entering the town, the scene changed:

> Then we came to St. Lo. . . . Not a building was left standing. The ruin is indescribable. A heavy dust covers piles of rubble, giving everything the same dead beige color. . . . [Here] the houses are too intimately exposed: their shattered staircases, scraps of furniture, and the jagged cross cuts of their construction and first-floor rooms filled with masses of tumbled masonry and stone . . . make them dead houses, and they should be buried. . . . In the center of the city lay the railroad station. . . . The tracks were twisted into fantastic shapes, rising in roller-coaster hoops. . . .

John O'Hara remembers that before the breakthrough, the Allies bombed St. Lo with as many as a thousand bombers at a time. As they flew over, they dropped little pieces of aluminum foil or magnetic paper —

chaff — to confuse the German radar. Smoke bombs were also dropped to mark the location of the enemy. Because of changing wind, some of the smoke from these bombs blew in the wrong direction, causing heavy casualties among our front-line troops as our bombers dropped part of their loads on them.

The idea of dropping chaff to confuse the German radar came from R. V. Jones, the scientist that British Wing Commander Scott-Farnie had assisted in finding the German radio beams. On one mission alone, 40 tons of the metallic stuff, shredded into 92 million strips, was dropped by 743 Allied bombers over German air space, sending their radar operators into a frenzy as they observed what appeared to be 11,000 bombers on their screens!

Near St. Lo, O'Hara and Lieutenants Hammer and Cox came upon a number of German staff cars loaded with explosives. A GI had hung a sign written on a V-mail form warning, "Don't _____ with this thing. It has a shell in it. Leave it alone." Booby traps were common and could lure you into sudden death. Later, some Ordnance men confirmed the GI's suspicions. A box of booby trap fuses had been found earlier with seven missing; in the German vehicles were the missing fuses.

It was in this area that the first mascot, a large Shepherd police dog, was adopted. Quickly the beast changed allegiance from German soldier to American soldier, but not to civilians or anyone out of uniform. Fortunately for three small local children, the men on duty were able to reach them just before being torn to pieces.

While inspecting the surroundings, Lieutenant Proctor met Monsieur Héon, a member of the French Résistance. He lived in a small village of charming houses populated mostly by refugees from Coutances. Whenever there was a threat of a raid, a pot of parsley was put in the window to warn the people. Proctor's diary describes Héon:

> [He] is an enormous fat man with handle bar moustaches and a great floppy straw hat which must be sewn to his head; he is never without it. . . . He is seventy-one. . . . He sent . . . a map prepared by the Germans and of which he made a copy. Thereafter, as he found out where the Germans had built their installations in Coutances, he prepared overlays on his copy, putting in simply marks on a blank sheet of paper, and sent that likewise to the BBC. He told us about a British Captain Wilcox.

This man spoke German fluently, and posed as a German officer. He stayed with M. Héon. . . . [His] plane exploded, and . . . he parachuted directly into M. Héon's front yard. M. Héon believes that the German race should be exterminated, that the Poles be given our half of the country and the Russians the other.

Moving on to Villers, our next destination, Lieutenant Proctor noted the complete devastation:

. . . Two old ladies, in black, stood before their house, what was left of it — holding hands, and just looking.

———————◄○►———————

Sometimes the days ran into one another without reference, and three months passed without the men of Detachment B having a haircut. Peter White, as a French-speaking officer, was ordered to scrounge around the Norman countryside, find a barber, and bring him back to camp. When he finished cutting, there were enough locks on the floor to stuff several mattresses.

The barber's wife had come along to see if she could get some shrapnel removed from her eye, but the doctors at the military field hospital, Lenox Hill, refused because they had been ordered to move out. It would have taken but a moment to put a little local anesthetic in her eye and take out the tiny piece of metal. Lieutenant White was furious. In his usual fashion of fighting for the underdog, he made it his personal mission to find treatment. After convincing the hospital to give him an ambulance and driver, he took the couple all over the countryside until a French hospital in LeMans agreed to help.

It was doubly distasteful to White to be turned away at Lenox Hill because the name conjured up images of New York's Lenox Hill Hospital at home. Many American hospitals had supplied volunteer doctors and their entire U.S. operating room staff to the war effort, who would set up field hospitals in Europe. These war-zone hospitals were named after the parent hospitals left behind. Moving with the front, these tent hospitals played leap frog with one another in order to allow each unit to get some rest. Even though postoperative mortality dropped from 60 percent in

World War I to 4 percent in World War II because of the introduction of blood, plasma, anesthetics, and antibiotics, the caseload was still endless and fatiguing and probably a bit of metal in the eye of a French madame didn't hold much importance to an exhausted doctor.

After the woman was finally treated, the barber suggested a short detour to visit a friend. They arrived at a lovely chateau, and during introductions the host asked Lieutenant White, "You are an American. Do you know Mrs. Justine Ward?"

With amazement, he replied, "She's my sister's Godmother!"

The Frenchman continued, "Is she rich?"

"I'd tell the cockeyed world she's rich!"

"Well, I'm her banker, and she had a house here, and when she left during the war, she gave me some money in order to keep on paying her servants."

After this astonishing coincidence, refreshments were served, and over drinks the ambulance driver got so drunk that he couldn't speak anything but his native French Canadian. The grandmother in the group spoke Norman French, similar to the driver's local dialect, so the two spent the afternoon in deep conversation.

When it was time to leave, the driver could barely stand, so Lieutenant White took over. With great difficulty he struggled with the jeep's little steering wheel and the strange gear shift. Becoming increasingly irritated, he gritted his teeth while listening to the grinding gears and his besotted "driver" chiding him. "What's the matter? Don't you know how to shift gears?" His subordinate's criticism only added to the tension as he drove through the pitch black night without headlights, a trip that he recalls as one of the most dangerous journeys in his military career — but not because of the enemy.

Every unit seemed to attract mascots — perhaps out of boredom or maybe just the simple need to be needed. It didn't matter if it was a human or an animal. It gave the men something personal to call their own in a very impersonal world.

René Paul Joseph Godard, claiming to be 14 but looking 10, attached himself to Detachment A, like a mascot, much to the initial delight and ultimate chagrin of Lieutenant Proctor. His story was that he lived

10 kilometers away and needed a place to sleep that night. After a break-
fast of pancakes, syrup, jam, and bacon, he was ours for life. Proctor's
diary recorded the event:

> It made his eyes pop. He spent the morning in the kitchen,
> had two showers and saw his first movie. He is a very nice little
> guy, and the men have a fine time playing with him.

By the third day, René Paul Joseph Godard became like chewing gum
stuck to your shoe:

> [He] is a pain in the neck. He has found a trumpet and has
> made a slingshot — and uses both with indiscretion. The air is
> full of noise and flying apples. He has also become possessive.
> His works are becoming a nuisance, so today he will be lured
> into a jeep and taken to the Civil Affairs people in Coutances,
> for what we hope will be a permanent and remote disposition.

Detachment B collected its own menagerie, thanks to Sergeant Milton
Rothenberg. It started with the acquisition of a plump juicy hen for dinner,
who instead became Henrietta the mascot. Rothenberg's soft heart added
a horde of fortunate chickens and dogs. Unfortunately, his tenderness
didn't seem to extend to humans, as Lieutenant Copp learned the night he
was readying the camp for an inspection by Captain Shaughnessy.
Shaughnessy was to arrive in the middle of the night. He would be coming directly from Detachment A, where everything was in top shape — a
hard act to follow. Copp tried to requisition a cot for the Captain to sleep
on and went to Rothenberg, who was the supply officer. Rothenburg poked
his head out of his tent, looking just terrible — half asleep, glasses side-
ways on his head. Copp started to ask for the cot, when Rothenburg cut
him off with a quick "No," turned around, and went back to bed. No one
remembers if Shaugnessy got a cot or where he slept. I imagine Detachment B's "mascots" slept better that night than did Shaughnessy.

◄○►

My unit, Detachment A, was getting restless again, and by the beginning of August 1944 we had received orders to break camp and move on

to Coutances near Coutainville Plage where we found ourselves at a beach. A beach — in August! Because standard Army gear did not include bathing suits, we frolicked in the nude like a bunch of innocent kids, ignorant of our comrades being slaughtered inland.

On our approach to Coutances the previous day, my buddies and I had spotted a deserted German ammo dump and now decided to check it out — an act that threatened another of my nine lives. Down a narrow lane lined by hedgerows we set off on our excursions like naughty little boys looking for mischief. We weren't denied. Stepping into a clearing, we came face-to-face with the muzzle of a well-camouflaged anti-tank gun set up to knock out anything and everything in its path. Moving quickly around it, we were tantalized by the enormous pile of ammunition crates. Each one was well constructed with sturdy rope handles and metal hasps. What wonderful storage bins they would make for our personal stuff!

The one-by-two-foot crates were stacked 10 to 12 high, and we were fascinated with what we might find inside. Like a bunch of curious children, we decided that the crates on top were not good enough and targeted one for each of us from the middle of the pile. Then, simultaneously, the same thought struck. "Suppose the site is mined or booby trapped?" Scrounging around the area, a piece of rope perhaps 30 yards long was located to help us "capture" the desired boxes without having the mass tumble down upon us and explode. Tying it to the handle of the first crate — mine, since I drew the shortest stick — we threw ourselves flat on the ground at the other end of the rope, tugging in rhythmic jolts until my treasure slid from the others. The process was repeated until there was a crate for each of us. How we had ever decided that our safety was determined by the length of the rope I'll never know. If the crates had been bobby trapped, the explosion would have destroyed everything within a half-mile radius, including all of Detachment A.

When we returned to camp to proudly show off our trophies, the realization of our naiveté hit us. If it had blown, there wasn't a rope long enough that would have saved us. How stupid we had been. Hadn't we learned anything from poor old Brian who had lost three fingers? It proved again that intelligence isn't a substitute for experience, nor does it change the feeling that young men have about their immortality. Later we joked about being a bunch of boobs with a booby trap. Fortunately, only part of that statement was true. From then on we had to lug our heavy, awkward boxes with us everywhere. Mine is currently in my garage.

Onward, we moved to Granville, and a few days later trucked to Avranches. From the road we were able to get an inspiring view of Mont St. Michel standing as a cathedral arising out of the ocean. The motor traffic was extremely heavy on the roads that entered Avranches because it was the key exit point from Normandy and everything and everyone funneled through it. The Allied storm that had struck Normandy on June 6th during OVERLORD had left ruin and rubble in its wake, but here, at Avranches, the only blemish on this spacious horizon was the charred corpse of an occasional tank or truck. Proctor's diary tells:

> It was at Avranches, too, that the most violent enthusiasm for Americans became evident. Not a soul on the roads failed to wave and smile; people stood by the roadside and held out bottles of wine and cider, begging us to take them; flowers sailed at us all the way.

As we bounced along in the back of the truck we became fascinated with what we thought were German mines being blown up in the surrounding fields. Then it hit us that it was enemy artillery fire and getting closer! "Step on it. Step on it. Get the hell out of here," we yelled as we all started banging on the cab and stomping our feet. It turned out that this was the beginning of a major counter-attack started by Jerry to cut our armies in half. Fortunately, our neighbors at Chalfont St. Giles, the 30th Infantry Division, managed to stop the attack, although for awhile they were surrounded.

As we approached Avranches the traffic increased, and we found ourselves caught in the logistics of an entire army trying to move through the town at one time. The intersection of the three major roads had been hit by a 16-inch shell fired from a U.S. battleship, and the huge crater had forced everyone to cautiously crawl around it in grinding low gear, and detour through the rubble of demolished buildings.

At an agonizingly slow pace we plodded, pushing through the mess. "Holy cow," someone yelled as our truck came to an abrupt stop. Not yet realizing the pun, we stared at a bizarre sight. To our left was a large, old gnarled tree surprisingly untouched by shellfire. It was very tall, and in its fork, about 30 feet up, was lodged a cow. Its four legs were poised in full stride, its eye staring. It was so undamaged that it was difficult to believe that it was dead, but the explosion had taken its life. Over the years I've met several veterans of the campaign, and frequently the one question they all have in common is, "Did you ever see that cow in the tree as you passed through Avranches?" It's an indelible image shared by many veterans of that Normandy summer of '44 — the summer of OVERLORD that changed the world.

————◄○►————

. . . When the imposing figure of General Hoyt Vanden-
berg, Commander of the 9th Air Force, showed up to com-
mend us for our work in the destruction of the German
19th Army staff, we were astonished.

Chapter Eight

Accolades and
Admonishments

S WE MOVED southeast from Avranches the landscape
changed dramatically. No longer confined by tall Norman
hedgerows, the roads widened and were flanked by sweeping farmlands and meadows offset by the black-green
contrast of copse and forest. Our next site of operation was
Parné-sur-Roc, a village between Laval and LeMans.

After setting up our equipment, the radio operators were put
quickly to work with a veritable flood of Wehrmacht radio traffic.
The picture emerged of an enemy in panic trying to regroup and
retreat. In the rush of events, the overwhelmed German operators
lacked time to encrypt and thus sent some of their messages "in the
clear." At the same time, we were breaking the coded messages so
fast that they were being decoded before they reached the German

receivers, creating that rare absurdity in warfare of knowing what the enemy is going to do before he knows it himself. One of these messages put a "scythe" into our hands — a tool that was responsible for destroying part of the headquarters staff of the 19th German Army.

The Record of Accomplishments for June 8 to October 26, 1944 states:

> Detachment "A" is officially credited with production of intelligence directly resulting in the destruction of 73 German aircraft, 3 probables, and 8 damaged. An outstanding example occurred during the German withdrawal from the South of France. Interception and decoding by Detachment "A" of enemy radio traffic indicated that COGNAC, BOURGES, and DIJON were centers of evacuation, and times of activity were noted. A single fighter sweep based on this information netted 33 a/c on one day alone. Succeeding sweeps resulted in further victories as well as the abandonment of the fields by the enemy.
>
> In addition, Det. "A" has produced much intelligence of a strategic nature, including battle order, scale of enemy offensive operations (fighters, bombers, night fighters, and reconnaissance) bases, serviceability of enemy air dromes, and results of enemy reconnaissance.

Detachment A had intercepted a desperate message one night, from German headquarters in Marseilles, requesting transport planes immediately. Our forces had broken out at St. Lo and were cutting off the German line of retreat. As soon as we decoded their reply, we knew how many German planes were being sent and when they would be dispatched.

After passing this information onto Headquarters, the American 9th Air Force allowed the German transports to fly into Cognac, Bourges, and Dijon and load up with their 19th Army Headquarters high-ranking personnel. Our fighter squadrons hovered in wait, then pounced, destroying numerous German aircraft and a significant portion of their 19th Headquarters staff. We received the following teletype message:

> 8 Ju 52's shot down so far at Cognac. Good work.
>   [Colonel] Dixon.

————◄○►————

As the war progressed, efficiency and order in the 9th Air Force did not necessarily develop with speed. By August 1944 Lieutenant Proctor was thoroughly disgusted with the situation and recorded in his diary:

> I called [Gangway — 9th Air Force Headquarters] . . . where I learned that his [Captain Edward Hitchcock, Intelligence Officer of 9th Air Force] office was closed; the Adjutant's office also was closed; A-2 was also closed. There was no billeting officer, and the operator had no way of knowing where the officers lived. So I tried the O.D. [Officer of the Day]; he was out inspecting the guard, but I did talk to the CQ [Charge of Quarters], a sergeant who told me that "It is dark as pitch here, and we can't use flashlights. The guard outside is nervous and has already shot five times tonight, so I don't dare go out hunting for Capt. Hitchcock.". . . . I asked them what they would do if an urgent message should come through at night; the answer was that such a thing had never happened, and they really didn't know what they would do. . . . What sort of Headquarters is this? These people would be better off in Kansas City. They were completely out of the war.

In war the right and left hands frequently got confused, yet this led to one of the most personally satisfying experiences of my military career. Scanning new material, I discovered a simple code substitution in five- and six-letter groups messaged from a Luftwaffe reconnaissance craft flying west over the Mediterranean. "J." Unusual, I thought. "J"? I mulled it over. . . . "J"? The ninth letter of the alphabet . . . but so what?

I made a guess, used intuition, and ran the configuration of the Mediterranean littoral. Suddenly I realized: "Ajaccio! The Corsican Port! That's it!" The scrabble finally made sense: "Large concentration of Allied landing craft in Port of Ajaccio." It referred to the preparation of the invasion of Southern France!

I brought the message to the duty officer, who in turn relayed the information to Headquarters. The message stirred 9th Air Force command like a stick swatting a hornet's nest. We were bombarded with queries. "What is all this? Invasion fleet assembling at Ajaccio? How? Why? Who? What?"

It turned out that SHAEF never informed the 9th Air Force of the projected invasion. Reason: "Not 9th Air Force's area of operation." One can understand the 9th's bewilderment. In Western and Northern Europe the 9th was the star of the show, the nonpareil of close ground support. The 9th could fly 72 squadrons against all comers. They could swarm an opponent with fighter bombers, strafe him with fighter planes — the works. But now they weren't informed of an invasion directed at Southern France? How does a *prima donna* feel when told her understudy will sing the lead role on opening night? Sometimes it was like we were dancing in the dark.

Breaking this seemingly unimportant message was the most significant personal coup I made during the war, but I didn't realize it at the time. Later I would have time to reflect upon my discovery and question what would have happened if I hadn't broken the code. How many things like this were missed that could have changed the direction of the war?

During my tour of duty, Detachment A often wondered whether our code breaking made a difference or if it was even recognized. After the war, Peter White, then a retired Colonel, stated:

> When guys who didn't go to West Point get to be officers commanding troops, they can get the job out, as we did, but they never learned one of the great functions of command, "Let each man know how he is getting along." While we were in the trenches we would have appreciated hearing that we had done useful work.

This was particularly true with our unit, and thus when the imposing figure of General Hoyt Vandenberg, Commander of the 9th Air Force, showed up to commend us for our work in the destruction of the German 19th Army staff, we were astonished. We had been told to prepare for an inspection, not a commendation. We were shocked. Never had anyone of such high rank visited us. Even Lieutenant Proctor felt awe:

> Yesterday General Vandenberg himself came out and spent an hour with us. . . . He was immensely pleased, and compliments flew pretty fast. He is on our side. . . . It is something of an hour of glory for us all. . . . Major Turkel is dancing for joy, and we feel pretty good about it too.

◄O►

For all the technology and power of the time, we had to rely a lot more on our instincts than is necessary today. The war was won and lost not by machines, but by men — men like those in my Intelligence group, the "special code-breaking unit." For this we were later awarded the Presidential Unit Citation personally promised by the tall, handsome General Vandenberg. The following March, my unit received the meritorious service plaque. It reads:

HEADQUARTERS
NINTH AIR FORCE
19 MARCH 1945

MERITORIOUS SERVICE UNIT PLAQUE

Charged with duties of a highly technical and exacting nature during the period June to December 1944, the 3rd Radio Squadron Mobile (G) carried out its mission in a superior manner. The successful execution of this mission required unusual knowledge of enemy tactics, and a high degree of keenness, patience and skill on the part of all operating personnel. In the performance of its outstanding duty the 3rd Radio Squadron Mobile (G) was instrumental in assisting directly in inflicting heavy losses on the enemy. Despite its frequent and rapid movements, problems of maintenance and supply, the 3rd Radio Squadron Mobile (G) consistently maintained and accomplished a superior performance on operations against the enemy during the invasion of France and subsequent operations on the continent.

By Command of Maj. Gen. Vandenberg

We were very proud of the citation and eagerly awaited promotions to go along with it.

Reminiscing in 1996, Fred Gottlieb said, "We were mighty proud of Detachment A breaking the code." Copp's words echoed his sentiment. "I knew that we [Detachment B] had to do well to keep up with Detachment A. We considered Detachment A quite great."

Declassified documents later showed that our efforts were well recognized by many outfits. On January 28, 1945, Commanding General

James Doolittle of the 8th Air Force sent a letter of appreciation to 3rd RSM:

> It is desired to express the appreciation of the Eighth Air Force for the material assistance rendered to the Eighth Air Force MEW [Microwave Early Warning] Station on the Continent by Ninth Air Force units. Ninth Air Force . . . did furnish such information, which has been a great value to the Eighth Air Force.
>
> "Y" messages showed that [the] enemy controller thought that the fighters were over the North Sea and the bombers over the Zuider Zee. . . . From "Y" information and MEW plots it became apparent that a large number of e/a [enemy/aircraft] were airborne.
>
> "Y" information helped identify our tracks and these e/a. On the basis of "Y" warnings, one group intercepted some 20 e/a in the Hanover-Quakenbruck area. . . .

This Letter of Commendation was TOP SECRET because it contained specific information regarding geographical location and number of enemy aircraft destroyed as a result of our efforts. In order to convey the message to his men, Major Harry Turkel ordered:

> The contents of the basic communication and [e]ndorsements are not to be posted but will be read to members of your command at formation under appropriate security precautions. It would be appreciated if you would indicate to each member of the Squadron present the pride and affection felt toward him by the Commanding Officer, 3rd Radio Squadron Mobile. . . . The defensive use of "Y" is equally important [as is the offensive], but it will never be known how many American aircraft and crews were saved by our timely warning.

As a result of our work, the 8th Air Force was able to combine its information with that of 3rd RSM and identify the aircraft on its radar screens. All of this came about over a chess game between Lieutenant Gottlieb and one of the officers of XIXth TAC. The TAC officer explained that his unit had Microwave Early Warning, but that there was trouble with it because all they could see were unidentified blips on the screen. They knew that the blips were planes, but they didn't know if they were German or Allied. Because Detachment D was monitoring all air traffic, and was able to identify a major portion of the bombers, Gottlieb suggested that they lay a phone line between the Detachment D Intelligence van and XXIX TAC. The result was great operational success.

According to Captain Shaugnessy, Generals Vandenberg and Patton said that the work of the 3rd Radio Squadron was "the best stuff" they had. Long after the war, in 1997, Colonel Edward Hitchcock, who had been Intelligence Officer at 9th Air Force Headquarters, substantiated their opinions when he told me that:

> 3rd R.S.M. information was more valuable to me than ULTRA. The decrypted messages and the German Voice radio intercepts were the most important components of my twice daily Intelligence briefing at 9th Air Force Headquarters.

This, indeed, was a time of both pride and frustration. As so many during the war had done, this small group, down to the last man, performed its best.

Life at this time seemed to divide itself into two worlds —
war and wonder.

Chapter Nine

Paris and I
Are Liberated

IT WAS EARLY SEPTEMBER — probably the 2nd — and I could hardly contain my excitement as we approached our next location and saw Paris in the distance. Riding into sunbathed France in an open-bed truck, I had been dazzled by my surroundings. The land was wide, rolling, and welcoming as it captured the sunbeams and robed itself in a cloth of gold. The magnificence of the Cathedral of Chartres as we approached Paris from the west in the late afternoon was mesmerizing, and it was blessed happenstance that we came upon it at the best time of day from the best direction. I had seen a castle, Mont St. Michel, and now a cathedral, Chartres.

At the time, I didn't know what a gift I had been given. It was marred only by the signs "*Contaminated by mustard gas*" posted everywhere to protect people from drinking out of the beautiful pools and springs. Water in the field was plentiful, but awful. Trucked to us in canvas bags with a spigot at the bottom, its temperature was as unpredictable as the weather; but we could always count on the flavor of the halazone tablets. I drank only to quench my thirst, never for pleasure. Maybe that was the point. Now I looked longingly at the crystal water that seemed to bubble everywhere — the forbidden spring.

To direct traffic to our next location, signs bearing our code name, Flap Able, dotted the area. The neighbors were curious and asked, *Qu'est ce, que c'est ce Flap Able?* When we replied that we were a communications detachment, they put their finger alongside their nose, *geste Gallican*, leaned toward us, and said, "You must be doing the same thing that the Germans were doing." Was our secret mission that obvious?

We reached our destination via the Red Ball Express, the 700-mile military highway that was supposed to be reserved specifically for supply transports whose orders were to stop only for loading, unloading, and refueling. This 24-hour, bumper-to-bumper traffic was a laborious grind, but still faster and more direct than the country roads. After leaving the main artery, we drove through a fairyland of forest surrounding Paris. The road was crowded with people returning on foot, bicycle, or jammed into coal-burning French trucks, with their belongings packed precariously into every conceivable kind of container. Later, when the rain began to pour down, they trudged on through muck and mire.

We rumbled through the village of La Celle St. Cloud and up a commanding hill, where we were halted by the gilded gates of Chateau Beaumont, the seat of the Comte de Beaumont, *La Chataigneraie* (Chestnut Grove). Captain Brinson and Lieutenant Davidson had arrived the day before to establish claim on the residence that Major Turkel had picked out for Operations headquarters. It loomed mysteriously in the twilight. On the double, we pushed open the gates and entered the interior splendor of parquet floors that echoed the presence of our heavy boots.

Our German counterparts, under Colonel Von Eick, had been here before us, sleeping, dining, and working within these walls. In their haste, they had left operational equipment, maps, and documents scattered throughout the ballroom and drawing rooms.

At the chateau we enjoyed the comforts that the Germans had prepared for themselves. The first floor ballroom had been converted into a theater where we later watched movies and held dances. Nelson, Irish, Nall, Wilson, Ludeker, Bright, and Worth formed a band with instruments they had brought from home. Our enemy had even gone so far as to build barracks divided into large private rooms (no foxholes here) accommodating three to six men, and had provided the ultimate in wartime luxury, showers and toilets! This was particularly welcome after living with a helmet washbowl for many months.

Unfortunately, the gorgeous art deco indoor marble swimming pool was filled with murky green, algae-laden water. The pool's filter was the only thing in the chateau destroyed by the Germans. The marble walls and pool were enclosed with a glass ceiling and tall windows on three sides, letting light drift in. In clear weather, warm rays of sunshine bounced off the water and the floor, turning the room into a dazzling display of multicolored sparkles. Overhead lights could be turned on to reflect their glow throughout the room and add a touch of magic. Oh, how we wanted to jump in.

Mortimer Proctor's diary resonates with the vivid memories of the chateau:

> . . . Up the stairway, on the mezzanine, the medics have set up shop. The officers have taken over the second floor. Hugh [Lieutenant Davidson] and I share a fine room — beautifully paneled, and with a chintz cloth covering in the manner of wallpaper. It has a large fireplace, and we have furnished it with twin beds, two overstuffed chairs; the whole room is carpeted. It opens on to a balcony shared by us and Captain Brinson and [Lieutenant Ivan] Fetter. . . . [The view] is perfectly beautiful. . . . S/L [Squadron Leader] Waters . . . was invited to inspect the chateau and was full of "Bloody incredibles," "Bloody marvelouses" and "Damned good shows," in his estimation.

Major Turkel attempted to care for the chateau as well as had the Germans, and ordered the china cabinet, which was filled with exquisite porcelain and crystal, to be secured, to prevent pillaging of the property. Captain Brinson remembers vividly:

He [Major Turkel] took a four-inch strip of tape and walked around that china cabinet five or six times, and he wrote thereon "Property of Major Turkel." Then he turned to me and said, "Captain Brinson, you're in command. You have a direct order that no man touch this cabinet." I did my best and I even placed a guard on this cabinet to carry out his orders but the next morning when we were trying to get all the men located, someone had gone in and removed all of the crystal. When Major Turkel found out about it he called me into his office and said, "I'm going to court-martial you. Do you understand Captain Brinson?"

"I understand, Sir."

From the standpoint of self-preservation I called Colonel Cody [Turkel's Commanding Officer who was head of all Intelligence at 9th Air Force]. "Sir, I did everything in my power to protect and carry out the orders of Major Turkel and I plead my case. If I'm court-martialed, I am not guilty."

Turkel finally cooled, but it left Brinson on edge for some time.

Settling down to work, the Intelligence section was told to use the tower, which provided a commanding view of the countryside — the Seine River and Paris to the east and the glistening gilded dome of *Sacré Coeur* — Sacred Heart Cathedral. To the west was St. Germain-en-Laye, a former royal hunting castle. The radio operators were sent below to revel in the splendor of the ballroom.

When my detachment had arrived at the chateau we were cautioned to maintain tight patrols in our area in the event of encountering isolated pockets of German troops that the Allied forces might have by-passed. For two nights we savored the comforts of our quarters, but on the third night our complacency was shattered with the stutter and bark of machine-gun and rifle fire from across the woods to the west. Captain Brinson, all absorbed with the responsibilities of command, quickly assembled off-duty personnel and formed us into squads to investigate what was happening. At the time, I remember thinking that Brinson's worry was bad form; but today I see it as a sign of superior intelligence.

Somehow I became squad leader for the venture. With only our carbines, we crossed the road and penetrated the woods to a distance of some 80 yards. It was a bitterly cold September night.

Darkness: the rain sluiced down; the mire was deep;
It was past twelve on a mid-winter night,
When peaceful fold in beds lay snug asleep;
There, with much work to do before the light,
We lugged out clay-sucked boots as best we might
Along the trench; sometimes a bullet sang,
And droning shells burst with a hollow bang. . . .

Had Siegfried Sassoon been here? Had he walked in my boots when he wrote "The Victory"?

As the chill penetrated my uniform, bullets suddenly began whistling overhead, clipping the branches above us. Diving for cover, I realized the danger in trying to reconnoiter in pitch darkness. Faced not only with the threat of enemy fire, but with friendly fire as well, I spotted the white bulk of a German pillbox at the convergence of two paths and led the squad to it. It was a vantage point from which we could observe movement, but as soon as we took cover, the firing stopped. Silence descended. Nothing happened. Staying just long enough to justify our patrol activity, we returned to the chateau and made our scanty puzzled report.

An explanation came with the daylight. The Russians who were being held in a nearby prison camp had been told that they were being sent home. Knowing that they would be branded as traitors for having been captured and would die in one of Stalin's camps, they rebelled. Triggered by vodka, or whatever happened to be at hand, they seized weapons and opened fire on the guards, trying to stop their transport back to the Soviet Union. Victorious, they had escaped, but the mellow men of Muscovy were eventually rounded up again by a detachment of MPs. We never knew what happened to them, but their fears were probably justified.

Those of us who lived and worked at the chateau realized what a magnificent jewel it was, and we were grateful for our time there. Whenever the Americans occupied a building in Europe, the host country was paid handsomely for its use. Thus was the case here. Rumor had it that the owner, Comte de Beaumont, was cooling his heels in jail on charges of collaborating with the Germans, so the place was for rent by the French government.

Although we appreciated the vast improvement in our living conditions, we were dissatisfied with a few things. The French always did prefer the bubbly to water, but when it came time to take a shower, we just wanted the plain stuff in full force. Since our arrival, all we had had was a slow trickle in the downstairs bath. Lieutenant Davidson finally went to the local water department and demanded a showdown, which produced no immediate results. "Why was it," he complained of *Monsieur L'Inspecteur*, "that the Germans had water and we don't?" In a hand-wringing flurry of protests, the authorities proclaimed their admiration, devotion, and love for the *Armée Americaine*, but no water. The Inspector adamantly claimed that the pressure was adequate up to the gates, and that was as far as his department was responsible.

Fortunately, with the chateau came Monsieur L'Mercies, a sort of career plumber. It was customary at that time in Europe to have hereditary occupations, and Monsieur L'Mercies' family had served in that capacity for many generations. He had devoted his life to the study of the plumbing within our abode. Stepping forward, he indignantly proclaimed to the water department that "his" plumbing was in excellent condition from the residence to the gates, and thus it was their responsibility to resolve the problem.

As Proctor aptly stated, "The French like to circumvent a problem and to savor the difficulties — to search them out, even before coming to a solution." Still nothing happened. Then suddenly a letter from *Monsieur L'Inspecteur* arrived, "In it he threw himself verbally to his rules, wept paragraphs, and promised that retribution would come to the man who had wronged us." It seemed that his agent had measured our water pressure at the wrong place, and now we had water everywhere we wanted. Cold water, but water.

The absence of hot water remained a mystery, but compared to our comrades freezing in foxholes through the worst winter in a quarter of a century, we felt very lucky.

Besides the initial water problems, we also had a number of other complications. As part of our rental agreement, French laborers were to fix the roads, cut wood for the winter, and hopefully mend a few broken window panes. The way these services were paid for was to deduct the amount that we owed from the total French war debt. By the end of the war it must have been a mind-boggling task to sort out stuff like this, but it was not our problem.

The first work crew arrived, and instead of Frenchmen, we got Arabs. After milling around for 15 minutes, they decided to strike for higher wages (19 *francs* per hour instead of 16.50). The terms were agreed upon and the problem was settled. The next day they arrived and demanded another raise. This time everyone was fired on the spot. The officer in charge journeyed to Versailles where he found a sympathetic ear — 30 strong, stable French workers and an English-speaking foreman. All was well, except for the continued lack of hot water.

Life at this time seemed to divide itself into two worlds — war and wonder. Social life at the chateau began on September 12, 1944, with an invitation to the officers for tea at Madame Bachelet's. The following night they were invited to Madame Allard's for what they hoped would be dinner, but instead, according to Lieutenant Proctor's diary, was

> . . . a very resplendent collection of cakes, scones and pastries, which she had somehow prepared in the one-hour-a-day period when the gas came on. The bulk of it she cooked over a wood fire. . . . [She] even got out some chocolates she had been saving for four years . . . and five bottles of champagne.

For her hospitality, the officers gave her a carton of cigarettes worth about $30 at prevailing prices. In reality, it was invaluable because cigarettes had not been available to civilians at any price. She cried. Lieutenant Proctor continued to reflect in his diary: ". . . a garden party is planned for Sunday. This isn't real! It certainly isn't war."

Not all the dinner parties around Paris were restricted to the officers. Life for the enlisted man could be delightful too. It's important to remember that the Intelligence unit of 3rd RSM was comprised of a rather unusual sort of recruit. Some came from educated backgrounds, speaking on a variety of topics and often in multiple languages. Others had social graces uncommon to most men of their young age, which provided entrée into the surrounding elite French homes.

Because the French were grateful and fascinated with us, invitations continued to be plentiful, and those who were invited eagerly accepted. At the disposal of the officers was Monsieur Cottet, a very polished, handsome gentleman who had managed the chateau's estate for decades. He now took it upon himself to see to our comforts, including social engagements.

The German occupation had had a dampening effect upon the local people because Jerry had simply taken what he wanted. The food shortage had become so bad that each person had been allotted only one ounce of meat per week, and children scavenged through garbage cans. The people felt that they were constantly being watched and harassed because they had to show passes everywhere they went. But with the invasion of Normandy in June, and the arrival of the Americans near Paris, the French came alive. The air was filled with the energy of expectancy and hope. We became the welcome recipients of their enthusiasm. It was an incredible time.

Being the officers in charge, Captain Brinson and Lieutenants Proctor and Davidson received the most invitations to the fancy affairs, and gorged on thick soups, stuffed tomatoes, rabbit, and apple pie — washing it all down with *Champagne Nature* — without fizz — and wonderful 1915 Burgundy, which was only 29 years old!

One of these dinners left a bad aftertaste. Monsieur and Madame Grosjean, who simply showed up at the chateau gates one day, invited the three officers to their house in La Celle St. Cloud. Never knowing if, and how much, food would be served, the men took the normal precaution of eating a little before going to the 9:30 p.m. dinner. Upon arriving, they discovered that a very elaborate meal had been prepared. Too elaborate, they thought. As Proctor said, it was a "masterpiece of black market manipulation." There was sausage with mushrooms, roast beef, assorted vegetables and fruits, cold meat pie, watercress salad, cheeses, and cake with a thick rich sauce. And with it all came the most extraordinary assortment of wines — three with each course, and refusals of refills were unacceptable as the host would sadly ask, "You don't like it?" Following the wine was champagne and plum brandy.

It was a "setting for funny business," said Proctor.

The host began asking questions about what our detachment was doing and said that Major Turkel had told him that we were doing the same kind of work as the Germans. This put the officers immediately on guard, because it was information Turkel would never have shared. It was all probably quite innocent, but it left the uncomfortable officers a bit wary.

The black market, as the elegant repast indicated, flourished everywhere and fortunes were made by individuals who previously had no avenue to generate large amounts of money. Lieutenant Davidson met one of the more successful French "entrepreneurs" outside the gates of the chateau talking about his postwar plans. "I'm going to get either a Cadillac or a Chevrolet." To a startled Davidson, he pulled out a drawer filled with *billets de banque* — *francs*. "I'm going to get *une voiture americaine* — an American car."

On August 25, 1944, the news of Paris's liberation spread rapidly. The surge of activity and excitement almost made my head spin as I reflected upon the past several months: the flight to London, the departure from Chalfont St. Giles, the road to Southampton, Omaha Beach, the breakout from Normandy. As I approached my twenty-first birthday I was participating in the experience of a lifetime.

Besides Paris, I felt liberated as well. It was at the chateau that I began my cigar-smoking career. Rations were always unpredictable, and there was an acute shortage of cigarettes and pipe tobacco. I had never been much of a smoker and engaged in a pack a week only because it was "the thing" to do; but with the lack of tobacco of any kind, my appetite increased. When the supply Sergeant announced that he still hadn't been able to get any cigarettes but did have a few cigars, I was intrigued. I lit up and found myself caught in the ambiance of the experience. It wasn't the cigar itself so much as the moment of pleasure it gave. It was like drinking fine wine in sparkling crystal or inhaling cognac as it rolled around the snifter. Peter White also remembers cigars from his days in London when he was offered a *Divinos Sublimos Excellentes Especiales*. I'm sure my introduction wasn't quite as *excellente* or *especial*, but I sure did get hooked.

The war and France changed my life permanently. Although I had studied French in high school, I had never done well with the language, barely getting Cs in my two years of study. Perhaps it was because of lack of interest, or the fact that ancient Spanish, not French, was the language of choice in my home while I was growing up. Now in France, the words suddenly began to flow. Egged on by my ego and my peers — *"Hey, Franco, tell her I like her"* — I became a one-man dating service for Detachment A. My popularity within the unit was at its peak as the overwhelming hospitality and sheer enthusiasm of the villagers of Bougival, Vaucresson, and La Celle St. Cloud hailed us as liberators. Heady stuff. I became my own best client and garnered for myself the irresistible charms of the pretty Christiane Lorthiois, daughter of a family of *haute bourgeois* related to Charles de Gaulle, considered the savior of France.

I first met Christiane's family in a local cafe when they, and other French families, were getting acquainted with the American soldiers. Dancing and singing the national anthems of each country, the "Star Spangled Banner," and the "Marseillaise," I also got to know my new buddy, John O'Hara.

The Lorthiois invited us to dinner at their home in Vaucresson on the outskirts of Paris, where we subsequently spent many enjoyable evenings. Upon our arrival that first time, we were asked our age, and being a bit older than John, I was seated to the right of Madame, the seat of honor. From then on we had dinner with them weekly, as well as on holidays, and I paired off with Christiane, and John with her fiery younger sister, Paquita, an exciting gypsy-like personality whose flame you feared would burn out prematurely, as it later did. I acted as interpreter, and we invited the sisters to our dances at the chateau, at which their father was always in attendance. I think it was more out of curiosity than the need to chaperone that motivated him to come along.

My social life expanded quickly, and I was invited to parties, dinners, and the "in" social events of the area. Enraptured by the adoration of Madame Lorthiois as she opened her home to me, I sometimes fantasized what my future might be like as her son-in-law. When I look back upon this wonderful time, I realize that John and I were two young men soaking up the attentions of a beautiful, voluptuous, and charming woman — a mature Marilyn Monroe. We adored her. She was a warm, gracious hostess that made us feel very grown up and very attractive. We responded to her attentions, and our affections for her were redirected to her lovely daughters.

Dinners at Maison Lorthiois were elaborate affairs, cooked and served by the live-in maid who prepared the delicacies of the black market. Since the time of the German occupation, Christiane and Paquita had ridden 20 to 30 miles into the countryside on their bicycles to barter for veal, ham, and other scarcities, with textiles from their father's factory. Their family had fled the north and had rented the large brick and stone house in Vaucresson to wait out the war, but still had access to the goods they produced, therefore providing them an excellent means of exchange. As winter approached, fuel was severely rationed so we were served in the only heated room of the house — the parent's cozy bedroom. A very nice tradition that I learned to enjoy immediately was the kiss on both cheeks, and the shaking of hands of everyone around the table before retiring for bed. John always thought that the double kiss gave him two for the price of one — a soldier's delight.

The Lorthiois were always kind and so complimentary that when they told John that his rusty high school French sounded like a "Spanish cow," he was not in the least offended and happily let me continue to interpret. I wonder how the sound of a Spanish cow differs from that of a French cow?

That freezing October of 1944 I took Christiane to the reopening of the Paris opera. As the audience sat huddled in overcoats, we watched *La Boheme* performed by shivering actors. Returning home, oysters on ice and chilled champagne in a glistening silver bucket awaited us. It was at that moment I first began to dream of becoming the son-in-law of Madame Lorthiois and living the romantic lifestyle she offered. I wasn't quite sure where I fit in, except that I was in love with it all.

The lively sisters talked openly with their mother, and my newness to the French culture created some confusion about what I was hearing. They discussed the single woman in the neighborhood, acknowledging that she had no husband but she did have a favorite dog. When I started to catch on to the innuendoes and realized that the dog was two-legged with pants, I was fascinated by the titillating sophistication of this family. I also quickly learned that although their conversations were more open than I had experienced at home, they had a strict moral code, no different from that of American families of the same social standing. Christiane and I continued to enjoy the feelings of youthful passion, but kept them under control. It was never discussed, but was tacitly understood, that our relationship would not go beyond an intense friendship — a friendship that exists to this day and extends to our families as well.

It was a strange sight to visit Paris during the war years. Fuel was so scarce that people had attached homemade, wood burning, stove-like contraptions — gazogenes — to the tops of their cars. The gazogene didn't produce much power, but it did get them slowly to where they were going, until it fouled up the engine. Perhaps the slowness of transportation was responsible for the development of the *pissoir*, an outdoor circular urinal surrounded with metal siding reaching from the neck to the knees. American servicemen liked to have their picture taken in one of these stalls. In some ways these outdoor facilities were preferable because they didn't have female attendants as did the indoor ones — a very inhibiting situation for a young man.

As December 1944 approached, my visits to the Lorthiois increased,

and on Christmas Eve the family took John O'Hara and me to mass at the
St. Cucufa church in Vaucresson. Weapons were supposed to be kept on
our person at all times, but this once we hid our guns in our host's garage.
It was the first time I had ever been inside a church, and the ceremony was
all the more moving because of the shadow of apprehension and fear cast
upon us by the latest enemy attack in the Ardennes. It drew soldiers and
civilians closer together.

I watched with wonder at the ecclesiastical ritual and felt the wonderful
energy of the Middle Ages resonating throughout the imposing structure.
When it came time for the collection, the priest tried to refuse donations
from the soldiers. As the plate reached John, he held it for a moment, gaz-
ing at one French *sou* that seemed out of place amongst the *francs* and
centimes. He had never seen such a small coin before because it was
worthless, much like a penny is today. But the sacrifice that *sou* symbol-
ized moved him deeply, recognizing that it was a gift from the heart of
someone who wanted to share regardless of how little. John gave 50 *francs*
that day, one American dollar — a handsome sum in 1944.

Candle flames flickered everywhere in the church and reflected upon
the walls, giving off a glorious warm glow. The Gothic edifice was packed,
and I was euphoric with the beautiful Christiane seated beside me. My
love of Browning surfaced again as his words rang in my ears:

> So, the year's done with!
>   (Love me forever!)
> All March begun with,
> April's endeavor;
> May-wreaths that bound me
> June needs must sever;
> Now snows fall round me,
> Quenching June's fever —
>   (Love me forever!)

After the service Christiane and I walked arm-in-arm through the snow
as the brisk bite of winter cut into our cheeks. In the warm, cozy atmos-
phere of Maison Lorthiois, the midnight feast was served, and we gorged
on every conceivable delicacy accompanied by the traditional holiday
blood sausage (*boudin*) and wine. John's fruitcake, sent by Aunt Mar-
guerite Miller, was a big hit, and Monsieur Lorthiois wondered if it would

catch fire if we tried to light it. Unfortunately, alcohol was not one of its ingredients.

At 4 a.m. I returned to my barracks for a very contented sleep. Christmas Day was celebrated in camp around the Red Cross Club mobile and the newly installed billiard table. Adaptations of Christmas carols and prayers proliferated, and the men found themselves composing and singing ridiculous little ditties to pass the time. You had to be a code-breaker to enjoy the full impact:

> Cheadle [in northern England, HQ of RAF Wireless Intelligence] is the shepherd.
> I do not want.
> It maketh my head to spin with numbers.
> It leadeth me to still-born kracs [the English "kraced" a code].
> It depresseth my soul.
> It leadeth me into paths of erasure.
> For its fame's sake.
> Yea, tho I walk in the snowflakes
> Of the valley of Chicksands [in Kent, where British voice interceptors worked]
> I shall know no orientation:
> For it is with me:
> It preparest a garble [a wrongly sent code unit, like a misspelled word] for me
> In the presence of the enemy;
> It anointest my head with corruptions;
> My index [of broken code words] runneth over.
> Surely Trumpet and Elgar [the names we gave to the codes the Germans used]
> Shall follow me all the days of my life:
> And I shall dwell in the house of
> Low low-grade noises [code breakers heard all sort of static noises]
> Forever.

> From *Kracer's Psalm* by J.A.W. (Unknown)

Before leaving Chateau Beaumont for good, soon after the New Year Detachment A received a commendation from Colonel Cody, Chief Signal Officer 9th Air Force, praising the value of our work. In support of the commendation was a teletype stating that on the basis of information furnished by our unit, American planes had bombed an airfield at Beauvais the previous August and had destroyed 16 Ju.52s. Our morale at that time had reached a new high with the praise from General Vandenberg, Commanding General, 9th Air Force. But still, no promotions.

In 1997 when Captain Brinson, Commander of Detachment A and the one responsible for getting us the promotions, was asked why there had been none, he replied:

> I assure you that I did everything that I could for my men, but in the Army you have what they call TO, Table of Organization, which authorizes what a CO can do in the way of promoting his men. No more, no less. And it stipulates how many corporals, how many sergeants, how many tech sergeants, and so forth. I do remember distinctly that in the TO it called for the operational personnel to be corporals. Why I don't know. They were making such a tremendous contribution, in my judgment, that they should have been much higher. Major Turkel and I talked frequently about trying to get the TO changed, but it was in black and white, and we could not deviate. It's just one of the mistakes that was made, and there were many, many, many mistakes.

We had no idea why the TO would be different for Detachment A than it was for the other detachments. Except for Paul Weiss who had joined Detachment A as a Sergeant, Corporal was the highest rank the cryptanalysts of Detachment A received. It did not help our morale that the motor pool, maintenance men, cooks, and truck drivers received stripes and higher ranks, as did the operational personnel of Detachments B, C, D, and E doing the same work that we were doing. Sometimes promotions were given for just showing up, doing your duty, or staying alive — but we were continually by-passed.

When I discussed this with in Jim Copp, of Detachment B, in 1997 he was astounded to hear that the code breakers in A had not been promoted beyond Corporal; and Frank Carnaggio, editor of *The Ninth Flyer*, the monthly publication of the 9th Air Force Veterans Association said, "I can't believe you were only a Corporal!" I couldn't either.

Official documents show consistent and frequent promotion of operational personnel in all other units. The Unit History of Detachment B states, "The number of men that were promoted totaled a little more than half the organization." This was for one month only. Detachment C's Unit History shows that "personnel changes consisted chiefly of promotions." Copp said that the Commanding Officers recognized what a morale boost promotions were and that every attempt was made to provide them for the men. This usually made the soldiers happy, except for the one case of Sergeant Kohlmeyer who got mad when he heard that he was no longer going to be a 1st Sergeant. He didn't like the sound of his new rank of Master Sergeant, thinking that 1st Sergeant sounded classier, and attempted to get Copp to demote him.

Regardless of the lack of promotions in Detachment A, we understood our goal and worked as a team to achieve it. Although we experienced moments of frustration, our time at the chateau was a time of purpose and plenty. We felt that we were doing a good job and our off-duty hours were spent in wonderment as the European world opened around us. For me, it was just beginning.

——◀○▶——

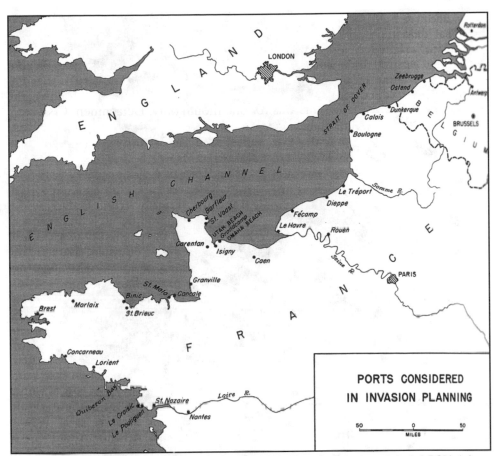

PORTS CONSIDERED

IN INVASION PLANNING

50   0   50

MILES

Arnold Franco was sent to England in April of 1944; his unlt, Detachment A, 3rd RSM, left Southampton and landed at Omaha Beach three weeks after D-Day. From *United States Army in World War II: The European Theater of Operations — Logistical Support of the Armies*, by Roland G. Ruppenthal, Vol. I (Washington, D.C.: Office of the Chief of Military History, Dept. of the Army, 1953).

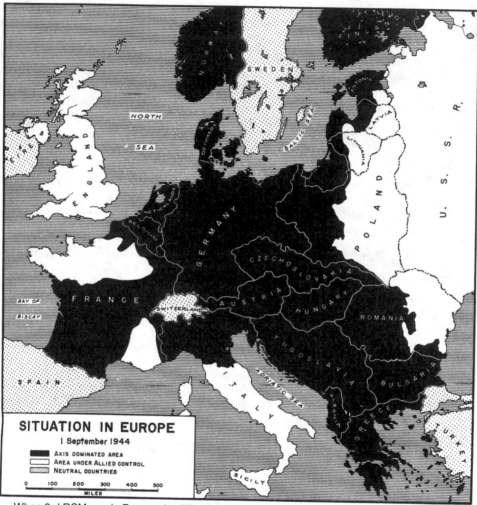

When 3rd RSM was in France, the Allies faced a grim "situation" in Europe. From *United States Army in World War II: The European Theater of Operations — The Lorraine Campaign*, by Hugh M. Cole (Washington, D.C.: Historical Division, Dept. of the Army, 1950), 7.

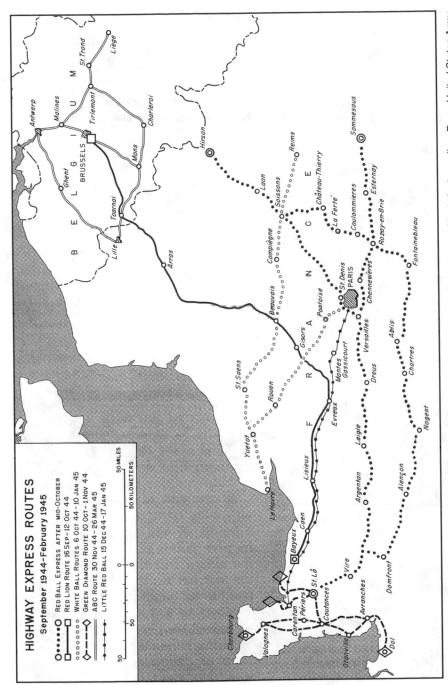

HIGHWAY EXPRESS ROUTES

September 1944–February 1945

○•••••○ RED BALL EXPRESS AFTER MID-OCTOBER
□—□ RED LION ROUTE 16 SEP–12 OCT 44
○○○○○○ WHITE BALL ROUTES 6 OCT 44–10 JAN 45
◇—◇ GREEN DIAMOND ROUTE 10 OCT–1 NOV 44
●—● ABC ROUTE 30 NOV 44–26 MAR 45
●●●●● LITTLE RED BALL 15 DEC 44–17 JAN 45

0   50 MILES

50   0   50 KILOMETERS

The routes of the Red Ball Express, the highways to be reserved for truck transport movement of logistical supplies. From *United States Army in World War II: The European Theater of Operations — Logistical Support of the Armies*, Vol. II, by Roland G. Ruppenthal (Washington, D.C.: Office of the Chief of Military History, Dept. of the Army, 1959), 136.

Privates Franco and Reeves arrive at Versailles, September 1, 1944.

A courageous French woman, head held high, returns to her street, 1944.

Corporal Albert Gruber in Paris, the second or third week of September 1944.

Below: A copy of Corporal Al Gruber's pass issued in September 1944 by Detachment B. B had installed their antennas atop the Eiffel Tower and for 10 days ran the place with the French family that traditionally held the elevator concession.

Albert J. Gruber   Cpl   32670827

SIGNATURE   GRADE   ASN.

LES AUTHORITÉS DE LA TOUR EIFFEL SONT PRIÉES DE
CÉDER AU SOLDAT PORTEUR DE CETTE NOTE LE DROIT
DE FAIRE USAGE DES SERVICES DE L'ASCENSEUR DE LA
TOUR POUR DES AFFIRES OFFICIELLES.

H. T. Silverstein
capt   ac

SIGNÉ.

Captain Ted Silverstein,
Paris, 1944.

Left: Some of
our German
predecessors
at the
Chateau
de la
Chataigneraie.
This photo
was one of
many items
left behind in
their hasty
late August
1944
departure.

Right: The calling card of Detachment A's predecessors at
the Chateau de la Chataigneraie.

LN. FUNKHORCH-REGIMENT WEST

DER KOMMANDEUR

The park (rear) view of the Chateau de la Chataigneraie, at La Celle St. Cloud. The front entrance and tower faced the Seine and Paris.

The marble swimming pool at La Chataigneraie, La Celle St. Cloud, September 1944. The pumps and other machinery had been destroyed by the Germans before they fled.

The tower of the Chateau de la Chataigneraie. The "X" marks the window of the large fireplaced room where the "code breakers" worked. On a sunny day it offered a splendid view of the Seine, all the way to the glistening dome of *Sacré Coeur* in Paris.

September 1944, on the grounds of the Chateau of the Comte de Beaumont at La Celle St. Cloud: from left to right, John O'Hara, Paquita Lorthiois, Ted Hansen, Christiane Lorthiois, Arnold Franco, Roger Barras, Monique, Annette, and Glen Lynch, of Detachment A, 3rd RSM.

The Lorthiois family with their American "stepsons" after Sunday dinner, Vaucresson, France, 1944.

Corporals Henry Hunger and Louis Piepmeier on either side of the 1938 Mercedes "liberated" by Major Harry Turkel and lovingly reconditioned by the motor pool at 3rd RSM Headquarters, Chantilly, France, 1944.

Ah, sweet Paris, to tempt a young man's fancy.

Chapter Ten

Madame Madam

PARIS! My appetite had been whetted by its horizon when we had approached Chateau Beaumont, and daily I had viewed the magnificent skyline from my work space in the tower. Finally I was here. Leaving New York with an insatiable appetite for politics and literature, and an education beyond my years, I had the illusion that I was quite sophisticated. I would soon learn otherwise.

In Paris I discovered a world I didn't even know existed — a romantic world of large-shouldered trench coats and extravagant hats. A magic in the air was untouched by the war, as the reality of my textbooks opened before me. Shop windows glistened and were reflected in the damp streets, just as the Impressionists had painted

them. I was dazzled. Like a child, I became aware of an enormous life outside Queens, New York, and I wanted to partake of it as fast as I could. It
was my first visit to this European wonderland, and my eyes and my
thoughts flitted from wonder to wonder. I took a moment to breathe in my
surroundings. I was *really, really* in Paris, and Isaac Rosenberg's "Home-
Thoughts from France" again brought me to this awareness:

> The spirit drank the café lights;
> All the hot life that glittered there,
> And heard men say to women gay,
> "Life is just so in France."

> The spirit dreams of café lights,
> And golden faces and soft tones,
> And hears men groan to broken men,
> "This is not Life in France."

> • • •

> Heaped stones and a charred signboard show
> With grass between and dead folk under,
> And some birds sing, while the spirit takes wing.
> And this is Life in France.

As I wandered the streets of the City of Light I found myself engaged
in window shopping — an activity I usually avoided. Absorbed by the
jewels and perfume behind the glass, I felt the presence of an elegant mid-
dle-aged woman standing beside me on the *Rue de Rivoli*. Tall and slim,
her face was veiled in black to match the couture lines of her frock. Her
attire was punctuated by a gold-handled walking stick. As we began talking, she became impressed that an American, especially a young soldier,
spoke such good French, so I was invited home for tea. Her residence,
resembling a New York brownstone, was a collection of large rooms that
reached through a lobby, one flight up, where the type-cast French maid
stood at the door in her short black skirt, white ruffled cap, and apron.
Here the Madame offered me the hospitality of a "madam," but being very
innocent in matters of this nature, I didn't understand.

As the afternoon wore on I became curious about the frequent ringing
of the doorbell and the constant activity of men coming and going.

Slowly I began to realize. The Madame noticed my increasing interest, and introduced me to her collection of lovelies. "I usually do not allow the military into my establishment. They get drunk and unruly; but you appear to be a very well brought up young man. You are welcome any time."

We finished our tea, and with our *au revoirs* I was determined to return as soon as possible. Thereafter, I was received frequently, carrying cigarettes, soap, food, liquor, and a variety of treats in exchange for a variety of their treats. The Madame and the girls were very fond of me. Ah, sweet Paris, to tempt a young man's fancy. I was beginning to feel a bit more confident.

————◄○►————

John O'Hara also absorbed Paris, through its landmarks — the Eiffel Tower, *Arc de Triomphe*, *Champs Elysées*, *Sacré Coeur*, *Notre Dame*, the *Louvre*. Later he attended *L'Opera* with his date, and saw Boris Godonov. Afterwards he took her to a GI nightclub and was embarrassed to find that the dancers weren't as covered as he would have liked for the eyes of a young lady. When he went to the *Folies Bergère*, it was with his buddies Phil Carpegna and Ralph Bloms. Years later he took his wife to see the show in New York, but the skimpy costumes no longer seemed as risqué.

The liberation of Paris several months earlier had been a turning point in the hearts of Europeans. Although Germany was not to surrender for another eight months, hope now hung in the air as the bells of the city had heralded the moment. When the news spread of the liberation, Claire Chevrillon, a member of the French Resistance wrote in *Code Name Christiane Clouet — A Woman in the French Resistance*:

> . . . then another sound, at first scarcely audible, suddenly swelled and seemed to come from everywhere at once. The bells, all the bells of Paris, were pealing forth together. They had been silent since the beginning of the Occupation. We had forgotten they were there . . . the whole city sprang to light. For a brief moment we believed the war was over.

On that memorable August day, jubilant crowds had swarmed the sun-bathed streets while the American Army stepped back and gave the French the honor of first entry to Paris. The Americans marched proudly down the *Champs Elysées.*

Major Turkel wrote to his children:

> Daddy and a lot of wild people entered Paris on August 25, 1944 with the first American troops. Oh, how happy everybody was. Everybody was kissing everybody else, exchanging cigarettes for tomatoes. . . . Daddy shook so many hands and kissed so many babies that he felt like a politician.

Liberated Paris was electric. People jammed the streets with arms reaching skyward as they jumped and shouted. Into passing vehicles they threw rainbows of flowers and wine, and stretched waving hands inside just to touch the American soldiers. Everyone was hugging and kissing, in a frenzy of emotion that had been bottled for many years. Now it was uncorked and bubbled over like the effervescence of sparkling champagne.

Lieutenant Peter White drove to the center of the city where everyone was celebrating. In his usual act first, think later enthusiasm, he jumped from his jeep and threw his arms around the closest, cheering damsel, conking her on the head with his metal helmet. Later he discovered that she actually was a distant relative. In 1995, when he returned to Paris for a family funeral, a woman approached him and identified herself as the girl he had bumped heads with 50 years earlier!

The day after the liberation, August 26th, a detail from 3rd RSM Detachment B was sent to Paris in preparation for the occupation of the city, and particularly the Eiffel Tower. Upon arrival, half of the detachment was billeted at the Swedish Pavilion, and the other half at the Spanish Pavilion, both part of the *Cité Universitaire* — an extreme improvement in their living conditions. Showers, however, were only available at 4 p.m. each day, and it seemed that the entire city bathed at once, reducing the water pressure to a dribble.

Subsequently, Lieutenant Copp formed a detail, putting Private 1st Class Abalos in charge, with a thrust of a broom and an order to "Police up the Eiffel Tower." With a broad smile Abalos replied, "Yes, Sir. I'll police it up like it's never been before." The next day, September 2nd, at 1900 hours, after the city was completely in Allied hands, Abalos' clean-up group began its work.

◄○►

From their landing in Normandy, until reaching the city, boredom from lack of amusements drove some of the men stir-crazy. But the Unit History of Detachment B records:

> In Paris there was everything a man could want, from hefty women for the red blooded men in this det. to a public library for the anemic type. Wines and liquors seemed to be in vogue.
>
> The "Big Parade" [came] staggering home after an evening's pleasure along the Rue Montparnasse. Back in Normandy, the boys used to holler because the only drink they could get was Calvados. In Paris there was enough of a variety to satisfy even a thirsty sponge.

Brothels and camp followers were everywhere in Paris, and with thousands of soldiers, the military thought that "sanctioning" their use would reduce the threat of local girls being bothered or even assaulted. In reality, the Parisians were generally quite willing to entertain and be entertained by the Allies.

When one of the jeep drivers was caught indulging in the services of a local brothel, he was arrested — not for taking his pleasure, but for leaving a gasoline-filled jeep in front of the House. With petrol a rare commodity and prostitution not, the MPs felt that his priorities needed adjusting. Later the young man was so tired from his activities that he fell asleep at the wheel. The jeep tipped over and his superior's helmeted head hit the ground. The Corporal was charged $275 for repairs.

Another unfortunate GI was enjoying himself in the same establishment, when it was raided for some reason or another. Jumping out the window, he found himself standing nude knee-deep in the middle of a snow-covered street. As he shivered, he realized the precariousness of his situation and dashed through the window of a flat on the opposite side. With every part of his body turning blue and numb, he quickly settled into the wonderfully warm bed of the building superintendent's wife. For a moment both were startled — just for a moment.

A third soldier was injured when he sprained his back in the local establishment and had to be sent Stateside. Not knowing how to properly document such an injury, the Army simply noted that he had been hurt in the LOD (Line of Duty)!

War created an artificiality to relationships, and Paris was no different.

There was an urgency that didn't exist in other times, and it is hard for those who haven't lived through such conditions to understand the emotional needs — needs that were manifested physically. In a world that seemed to have lost its humanity, the mere touch of one human by another, a lingering look, or a moment of tenderness, knowing that there might not be another, meant so much to the soldiers and to the women who were left behind.

———◄o►———

Acquiring the Eiffel Tower, the highest point in the area, for the installation of a radio antenna for 3rd RSM, was not as easy as had been hoped, nor did the resistance come in an expected way. Major Turkel had to apply a great deal of pressure to get permission to set up in the Tower, and it was considered a major success when it was granted. Built in the late 1800s, with a hydraulic elevator, the running of the elevator and access to the Tower had been in the hands of the same French family since its construction. But when Detachment B arrived to set up the antenna, the family simply said "No."

When the Germans had occupied Paris they had put armored plating around the top of the Tower and had used it as a spotter station. Now, after the liberation, the family wanted the Tower back; but Lieutenant Copp was just as firm. After lengthy and heated negotiations he gained entrée and ordered the repair of one elevator. Then passes were made out, with General Dwight Eisenhower receiving one of the first. The GIs became constant tourists to this historical landmark and all sorts of new problems arose as high-ranking military arrived without passes, demanding to go to the front of the line. Copp's first night in Paris was spent atop the Eiffel Tower guarding the prized military installation during a 24-hour shift — not so much from the Germans, as from other Americans that might "hanker" for the spot.

Special Tower passes were given to Private 1st Class Milton Rothberg and his buddies to climb to the top and photograph panoramic views of Paris from a variety of angles. Rothberg took some of these shots by hanging onto the railing with one hand and heels while holding the camera with the other and snapping the shutter with his teeth — not an activity for the fainthearted. While observing the entire city from above, the group noticed a parade near the *Arc de Triomphe* and immediately set off to photograph whatever it was all about. It wasn't until the film was developed that they realized their unbelievable achievement of getting within three feet of General Charles de Gaulle, General Eisenhower, and Air Marshal Sir Arthur Tedder while Ike was receiving thanks from the French Forces of the Interior (FFI) for the liberation of Paris!

After getting settled at the chateau outside Paris, Lieutenant Proctor wrote:

> How I hope that the whole job is done this time, that Germany is occupied and that no half-way peace terms are drawn up. The wretched cries about the harshness of the last treaty, which "drove Germany to fight for her life" should never be heard again. Neither should Germany. Lt. Ivan Fetter went to Paris the day before yesterday, and confirmed the reports that the whole city is alive with joy now that the poison has been removed.

For each soldier, Paris was a special time, but to see it in the glory of her liberation was an indescribable moment. To be the liberator in a city that had been put to sleep by Hitler's shadow, left many young men overwhelmed with victory and with a feeling that they could conquer the world.

————◄o►————

. . . I discovered what it meant to be a Jew. My connection was inescapable . . .

Chapter Eleven

Mein Kampf — My Struggle

NOT ALL MY TRIPS into Paris from our headquarters were pleasant. During the war people disappeared so easily. Without a trace, a life seemed to merely cease. My father's uncle had not been heard from in three years. He had owned an apartment in a very nice part of Paris, which I quickly located. The concierge, a pleasant woman, chatted comfortably with me in French, but her response to the whereabouts of my relative brought a disgusted, "Oh, *him*, the *L'Israelite* (the Jew)." Her obvious anti-semitism destroyed my naiveté that all was well for Jews outside of Germany. Later I searched out another Jew, and the experience redirected my life.

In New York, an old friend of my father's, asked me to inquire about his relatives, a married Sephardic couple — Jews whose ancestry traced back from Spain and Portugal. I searched the city for the address, passing through bleak, ugly streets and dark quarters that I would never have ventured into except for my obligation. Finally, I located the miserable residence in a barren wasteland of rubble, devoid of anything green. Time slowed. I waited, trying to find the courage to raise my knuckles to the peeling door. Fearing what existed on the other side, I took a deep breath, longing to return to a saner world. Hoping the flat would be empty, I knocked. A man about 40, haggard and prematurely gray of hair and face, stood before me. His eyes were dulled by shock, his skin deeply lined. Assuming that the woman beside him was his wife, I inquired, but she shook her head. Emotionless, they invited me in — no curiosity, only a lethargic, disinterested response. I felt that I was watching a moment of stop-action film being created before my eyes that I couldn't quite grasp. The room was nothing more than a hovel with no purpose other than to shield its inhabitants from the chill of the outside world. As I sat on the edge of the dirty rumpled bed, the only place for a visitor, the one faded and tattered curtain hanging on a string let slices of dull gloom filter through the mud-streaked window and fall across my knees. Something began to seep into my consciousness, something I was yet to recognize but could intensely feel. For the moment I buried it and returned my attention to the man.

"My family," he said, "my children, my wife," and then he stopped. His shoulders hunched forward, his head sunk. For a moment he was unable to go on. The silence became so heavy that breathing seemed difficult for us both. In jagged pieces he told the story. After the German occupation in 1940, he and his family had fled into the countryside and had been able to evade discovery for more than three years. While out scavenging for food, he was picked up by a forced-labor gang and hauled off to the coast where he was put to work building fortifications for the Germans against the coming Allied invasion — what would be called the "Atlantic wall."

When the Normandy invasion struck there was so much confusion he had been able to escape. Germans were frantically trying to reinforce their units while the Allies were bombing from the air.

Everyone then became his enemy. After a harrowing trek through the forest trying to avoid capture by the Germans and injury by the Allies, he finally reached his village. Eager to see his family, he soon discovered that everyone he knew had been swept up in a raid by the *Milice*, the pro-Nazi French Fascist organization that was the instrument of the Vichy government, outside of Paris. Later, the man was informed that his family had been consumed in the furnace of the Holocaust. And now he was trying to console himself with another woman. From the look in his eyes, I felt that consolation would never come.

After awhile we said our good-byes with no invitation to return. The door closed behind me.

At that moment my life changed as I discovered what it meant to be a Jew. My connection was inescapable as I stood in the cool night air, recalling Wilfred Owen's lines from World War I, "A Farm Near Zillebeke":

> Black clouds hide the moon, the amazement is gone;
> The morning will come in weeping and rain;
> The Line is all hushed — on a sudden anon
> The fool bullets clack and guns mouth again,
> I stood in the yard of a house that must die, . . .
> Black clouds hid the moon, tears blinded me more.

Man must be mad, I thought. What I was seeing here firsthand was leading me to confront my own heritage. "A life that is not examined is not worth living," Socrates had said. I was beginning to examine.

As the war progressed, persecution of the Jews moved from theory to reality in my world. In America I had recognized the threat from an early age, but now I was face-to-face with something larger than just a personal slight or threat. Discovery of what was going on with the Nazi command came from my own direct experiences and information picked up through Intelligence channels. Initially this information had been so horrific that I had been unable to comprehend its scope. But denial was no longer an option. Hitler was real. The Holocaust was real.

As the conflict escalated, occupied France had slowly and insidiously imposed increasing restrictions upon the Jews, beginning with the definition that a Jew was anyone who had three Jewish grandparents or two Jewish grandparents and a Jewish spouse. Once identity was established, he or she could not teach school, run for elected office, nor be involved in radio, film, theater, or publishing.

Though these conditions had been limiting, they were livable. But by the time I had reached France, the rules had been expanded. Now a Jew was defined as any person with a Jewish parent or two Jewish grandparents and who was neither Protestant nor Catholic. The squeeze was on.

The appalling demands made life in France intolerable. The chest-worn yellow stars marking my brothers' identity had to be purchased with precious ration coupons and sewn securely in place. Not understanding the significance, the children were excited to have a little decoration in their drab world. Food could only be purchased at certain times, usually between 11 a.m. and 12 noon, after supplies were most certainly gone. Cafes, theaters, parks, main boulevards, and public telephones and benches were *verboten*. Later, Jews could use only the last car in the Metro, and private radios and telephones were confiscated. In *Code Name Christiane Clouet*, Claire Chevrillon writes, "The French people were either gagged or collaborating."

The whole picture became painfully clear and forced me to focus on my own religious background and define who I was within the context of a larger picture. My increasing indignation about what I saw and learned became so disturbing that I internalized much of it and was unable to speak of it until after the war. The signs, *"Interdit aux Juif's," "No Jews Allowed,"* reminded me of the signs for "Whites" and "Coloreds" that I had seen during training camp back in the States.

The Sephardic Jew of Turkey and the Middle East had come under strong French cultural influence prior to the First World War. This was particularly true of members of my family. A few had moved away from their heritage and chose to appear as Frenchmen, so much so that they spoke fluent French and affected Gallic airs. Some of their friends even changed their names to conceal their ancestry. All of this was probably due to a desire of the younger generation to escape the restrictions of orthodox Judaic tradition — the family, after all, boasted three rabbis.

Their means of escape was the *Alliance Israelite Universelle*, an institution originated by the French Jews in the 1860 France of Napoleon III. The purpose of this organization was to protect the Jewish cultural values in Europe, Turkey, and the Middle East from invasive assaults, such as the kidnapping of children and forced conversions to Christianity. The *Alliance* was formed to combat this. Schools were established to introduce Jews to a full spectrum of study beyond the confinement of the Talmud. Over the years, the A.I.U. became an educative end in itself — it moved from rescuing the Jews from peril to providing a more global education for the people.

In the autumn of 1944 I contemplated the earlier choices my family had made and thought about how I had never emphasized my Jewishness nor paid much attention to those Old Testament milestones marking the holidays. Although I was aware of being a Jew, I had never fully realized what it meant for the individual, Arnold Clement Franco, until I confronted it head-on. As the war now presented a moment in which to reflect upon my past and my future, my feelings turned bitter. The atrocities and horrors could no longer be ignored. An insane leader of a major European country had determined that all of my kind — and, if given the chance, that I, too — was to be exterminated.

Caught in the crosshairs of my lineage and religious traditions, social acceptance in my own country suggested that I should disguise my identity. I had grown up with intolerance and violence in a land supposedly free from such injustices, and now saw firsthand how *bad* bad could really be. When I finally accepted that the Jew "over there" was the Jew everywhere — of which I was one — I understood that I was fighting the war as much for myself as I was for others. Hitler was forcing me to become a Jew.

The hell with it, I decided. I refused to live a hypocrisy. I would marry a Jewish girl and instruct my children in the tenets of the faith.

It was then that I fully realized I could not let my friendship with Christiane develop into anything deeper. Although I felt comfortable with the family, I knew that to marry into its foreignness and its lifestyle was ultimately not for me. Near the end of the war I was to read in a camp newspaper an article about the American presence in Germany — that as long as we stayed we would simply be superimposed upon the surface of its life like oil on water, never fusing. This put into words what I had realized earlier in France regarding my relationship with Christiane.

When I had left America to enter the war, I felt that I was actually fighting a crusade — one I had been destined to enter. Years later, a therapist interpreted my feelings as a Christ syndrome — I thought I had to give my life for the sins of society so that it could be redeemed. In France, I discovered who I was and who I wanted to become, and how Rudyard Kipling's poem "The Recall" applied to my future:

> I am the land of their fathers,
> In me the virtue stays.
> I will bring back my children,
> After certain days.
>
> Under their feet in the grasses
> My clinging magic runs.
> They shall return as strangers.
> They shall remain as sons.
>
> Over their heads in the branches
> Of their new-bought, ancient trees,
> I weave an incantation
> And draw them to my knees.
>
> Scent of smoke in the evening,
> Smell of rain in the night —
> The hours, the days and the seasons,
> Order their souls aright,
>
> Till I make plain the meaning
> Of all my thousand years —
> Till I fill their hearts with knowledge,
> While I fill their eyes with tears.

It seems that tears were everywhere now. And tears brought forth so many questions. How would I face the enemy now that I had faced myself? Would I see him as a part of a hated race? And if we were victorious, what kind of victor would *I* be? What kind of man would *I* become? What kind of mark would *I* leave behind?

————◄○►————

Although this is a memoir of the men of 3rd Radio Squadron Mobile (G), it is difficult to ignore the stories of those we were fighting for — the

millions whose lives were forever changed by the events of World War II
— those who endured horrendous tortures and went silently to bullets and
ovens.

The experiences of my cousin, Elisa Franco-Hasson, a beautiful young
girl sent to Auschwitz, is one of these stories. In her book *Il Etait une fois
l'Ile des Roses* (*It Was Once the Island of Roses*) she writes:

> Scarcely arrived [at Auschwitz] we had to undress and in the
> nude we were shaved by men; hair, armpits, pubic area, all was
> done. As we were already full of lice as a result of being
> crowded in the train for so many days, shaving made sense in
> its own way, but this was, above all, part of their program of
> humiliation. To submit to this degradation filled us with rage
> and shame — we had lost all personality. But, at the same time,
> looking at one another, we couldn't avoid bursting into laugh-
> ter, albeit a very nervous laughter. It's just that without hair we
> all had boy's heads. And some of us, knowing the families of
> our companions, exclaimed, "Why you look just like your
> brother," or "Look, it's her father all over again." In effect, we
> had in front of us our brothers, fathers and uncles.

Elisa lost her youth in that camp — her only memento from that time,
a brittle, yellowed scrap of paper. After being released, she sent a telegram
to my father Leon Franco, dated January 1945, telling him that she was in
Rome and needed a winter coat. Being the historian that I am, I preserved
the telegram and returned it to her years later. She relates:

> I keep it as a precious relic . . . of that period. I have absolute-
> ly nothing [else] to remind me of my past (the time before and
> during camp). Not even the slightest item, scrap of paper,
> photo, etc. Nothing to recall my life before the camps.

———◦———

In the winter of 1944, Dr. Alex Shulman, a neurosurgeon, was stationed
in Belgium. As the Battle of the Bulge raged around him, he was treating a head wound. A filthy young German boy, perhaps 14 or 15, had
avoided capture by hiding in a barn for several weeks after being cut off

from his unit. He had a terrible gash covered with dried blood and matted hair:

> As I took him to the operating room, he started to cry. . . . All I did was get a basin of hot water and some soap and washed his hair. Here was a captain in the US Army washing the hair of a little German boy. . . . Then he really started to cry. "What are you crying about?" [I asked in German.] "They told me I'd be killed. And here you are, an American officer, washing my hands and face and my hair." I reminded him that I was a Jewish doctor. . . .

What happened in the war continues to touch people's lives today. In 1995, one year after the Northridge, California, earthquake, the *Los Angeles Times* requested stories about the experience. When the quake hit, a woman who had treasured and protected the only possession her grandmother had been able to bring to America from Nazi Germany yelled, "Save Mutti's bowl." Although it had survived the Holocaust and the trip to America, the bowl was shattered in the 1994 quake. Devastated, the granddaughter reverently collected the pieces. Realizing that the fragments were a part of her grandmother who had recently died, she was unable to throw them away. She commissioned 14 sculptures of Mutti, one for each family member, and had placed in the lap of each sculpture a piece of the bowl.

In 1977, at the age of 53, I was a Bar Mitzvah.

As Detachment C continued to move through the French countryside, the mark of death had sought out everything. Dead horses were still hitched to the wagons they had been pulling, . . . their punctured carcasses lay rotting next to the unburied dead enemy. . . .

Chapter Twelve

The Best of Times and the Worst of Times

WHAT DOES THE ENEMY LOOK LIKE? Is he tall, squat, hulking? Is he single or married? Does he have children? He remains faceless, unidentifiable except for the rhythm he uses as he taps out Morse Code with his key.

———◦———

Commanding Officer Major Turkel, 3rd RSM, wrote home:

I don't think I have ever had such an interesting job in my life. . . . Never since I came into this Army have I had so many headaches, but that phase seems to be over, and we're really cookin'.

He acknowledged that "Even my enlisted men are a really brainy lot," and this created a challenge in keeping them occupied and out of trouble.

Problems were as varied as the possibilities and one arose when Y Intelligence was "too" efficient, receiving and breaking the German transmissions before the Germans got their own messages. This had once resulted in Detachment C moving ahead of both the enemy and its own protective infantry.

Having been informed of the location of a German Y unit, Lieutenant Heinrich of C had moved his men toward Rennes, hoping to get hold of secret documents and perhaps even capture a few German counterparts. On the heels of Jerry's departure from Chateau de la Massais near Rennes, Heinrich found only an empty three-story mansion. He radioed Major Turkel of the situation and then began inspecting the premises in more detail. In their haste, the Germans had left behind a collection of records revealing the complete administrative set-up of the immediate German Air Force signals installation and its ancillary and associated units. It was a gold mine of information.

During this time, Corporal Ropp, of Detachment C, was out exploring the countryside, when unexpectedly he came upon some German soldiers camped in the protective denseness of the forest. Having been separated from their unit and knowing that their war was coming to an end, the demoralized group was wandering around trying to find a safe way to surrender. Not understanding this, the GI quickly retreated back to the chateau and sounded the alarm that the Germans were only five miles from the chateau and moving their way. This shocked the officers in charge when they realized that they had accidentally moved the detachment past the Germans and were now ahead of them without protection!

Major Turkel had just arrived and settled down with a bottle of champagne, never expecting that a German advance would turn into a surrender right at his front door. The Unit History states:

> Detachment C had its first experience with taking prisoners of war. Soon after lunch one day eight bedraggled German soldiers suddenly appeared on the hillside above the chateau. Corporal Ropp, unarmed and going about his maintenance

duties, was the first to discover them. Reacting quickly, he pretended to be pointing them out to armed men behind him. The German soldiers came on into the courtyard of the chateau saying they wanted to surrender. They were fully armed and had a sufficient supply of ammunition, but, believing the superman myth, they chose not to use their weapons. Their first desire was water, both for drinking and washing purposes. These prisoners were taken to a P/W camp near Rennes . . . [which] opened that day, and [was] not expecting "guests" quite so quickly.

Later, Major Turkel wrote to his children:

> Daddy was sipping some bubbly water with his No. 12's on a desk when a sergeant stuck his head in a window and said, "Sir, here are eight armed Germans coming through the gate." Your Daddy nearly choked because French water is so bubbly, and he went out the door like a bat going places. . . . As he swung out of the door Daddy yelled *Achtung* which, in the German language, means "Pay attention," and some of the Germans raised their hands as if they wanted to pray and some of the others saluted, so Daddy saluted, too, because HE didn't feel like praying just then. Then Daddy shouted *Reihe machen* which is not a good German order, but in plain German language means "Make a row." Then Daddy made a mistake. He yelled *Abweise zeigen* which means "Show your identity cards." There was necessarily a bit of fumbling around before they could produce them.

For a brief time, Detachment C enjoyed the beautiful flower and vegetable gardens on the Chateau de la Massais' extensive grounds, the large, airy rooms with sinks, flush toilets, and electric lights, a water-filled moat, and the unit's first mascot, Pete the Pigeon, plus a recreation center, hospital, barracks, and an interlocking defense system added by the Germans.

From the chateau, Detachment C moved to Monfort through Laval and Le Mans, where the Americans were able to see the devastation its own Army had caused to a rapidly collapsing military regime. The motor transport that had been attempting to retreat and escape back to Germany was destroyed with deadly accuracy. Its burned-out passenger and freight vehicles littered the picturesque tree-lined roads, leaving monuments of defeat.

In Monfort, Detachment C picked up three mascots: Character the Cat and two German police dogs, Tom and Fifi, who were suspected of being spies in dog's clothing, and whose main function was to determine the quality and quantity of food that was going to the dogs in the U.S. Army. Major Turkel wrote to his children that he also encountered a dog in the vicinity, and this one caused a case of mistaken identity. "Daddy thought it was a German, and it was only a German dog, which is pretty much the same thing." Pete the Pigeon had stayed behind at Chateau de la Massais after deciding to take up permanent residence there.

Lieutenant Proctor had showed up at Rennes scavenging for German equipment that had been so hastily left behind, but the only things he procured were a few tables, one much desired folding steel cot, and some wonderful food.

> Ah, what beautiful melons! The first in nearly two years. . . . The road was filled with shell holes in spots, and I nursed three dozen eggs through it all until the very last, when the one casualty occurred.

As he traveled, he observed that the surrounding landscape

> . . . [was] scarred equally from the shells of 1914-18 and those of the past months; the moss on some of the ruins tells which ruin belongs to which war. It is an odd thing, driving through these old battlefields which have been brought to life by new battles.

As Detachment C continued to move through the French countryside, the mark of death had sought out everything. Dead horses were still hitched to the wagons they had been pulling, and their punctured carcasses lay rotting next to the unburied dead enemy whose distorted faces and twisted bloodied bodies held the pain of their violent end. The road was littered with empty artillery cases, ammunition boxes, and fake enemy tanks that had been built over farm wagons and camouflaged. The battle that had been fought with warm blood and cold courage left nothing untouched. Signs of Americans also littered the landscape — empty K-ration boxes, cigarette packages, and Allied leaflets thrown from planes instructing the German soldiers on how to say *ei surrender.*

In Foulquemont, Detachment C found adequate lodgings at the site of a coal-mining operation, about 15 miles due south of the Siegfried Line. On the fourth and fifth floors of the administration building, the men set up operations and enjoyed respite from the constant noise of the outside world and their cramped British vehicles that seemed designed for very short men. Except for the burning eyes and uncontrollable tearing from back-winding stoves, the living quarters were a welcome luxury, even though the logistics of going down six flights of stairs, 200 steps, to the dining room and latrine in the basement made everyone consolidate their needs.

But the absence of sunlight at Foulquemont wore on morale. Morning after morning the men opened their eyes to a gloomy, heavy gray sky and felt the moisture ooze out of the air and seep through their uniforms. The monotonous weather and miserable mail service worsened as winter deepened. The thought of spending Christmas in a cold, smoky concrete office building gave none of the warm glow of holidays remembered, but the men of Detachment C were fully aware of how much better off they were than the thousands of fellow soldiers who were literally battling for their lives against odds elsewhere in the numbing cold. Even the small amount of canned frankfurters, raisin bread, and K-rations was appreciated.

On Christmas Eve, most of the outfit spent their time packing stockings instead of filling them. They had again received orders to move out. False rumors of invading German paratroopers had filtered through the American units, causing the men to become more and more anxious as numbers dwindled with the reassignment of each echelon. Now the guarding of the large building was left to a handful of men.

At Detachment B, Major Ted Silverstein was occasionally off in his jeep inspecting or assisting his men. In some places there was a standing order that all jeep windshields had to be left down to avoid reflection and possible spotting by the Germans, but in France the order was the opposite, to protect the occupants from being decapitated by an enemy's wire drawn across the road. Keeping the windshield up, however, created a hazard, because it was impossible to keep the glass clean, making visibility extremely difficult. While coming back from Luxembourg City, Silverstein was pulled over and asked to wait as a man went into his house and got a potato. After cutting it in half, he rubbed the windshield with the cut side — a small but kind gesture. It not only cleaned the glass, it repelled the dirt for the rest of the journey.

Vehicles seemed to plague Silverstein throughout the war. When it was over, he found himself in trouble because he had to leave his truck in Jalhay, Belgium. Whenever a soldier was assigned a piece of equipment, he had to sign for it and was responsible for its care. At Jalhay, Silverstein's truck was shot up by the Germans and became inoperable. When he left town, there was no alternative but to leave the truck. It was a real Catch-22 when he tried explaining to the brass that there was no way to drive the vehicle, and they merely cited the rules of the Army that he was responsible for returning it regardless of condition!

While we were luxuriating at Chateau Beaumont outside of Paris, Detachment D found itself a cozy chateau of their own at La Jonchere not too far from us. Having lived several days in transient camps with nothing but K- and C-rations, they enjoyed their first hot meals, washed their clothes, wrote long delayed letters home, and scavenged through the miscellaneous junk the Nazi occupants had left behind. A various assortment of souvenirs, ranging from mattresses to copies of Dr. Goebbel's *Das Reich* found their way into duffel bags and packages sent Stateside. There was also an assortment of wine, but this was drunk cautiously because the Germans liked to remove the corks and top off the bottles with a little Hun piss. Unfortunately Detachment D only got to stay there a week, but before they left every man got to enjoy cider and apple tarts provided by the baroness, the countess, and the marquis.

Although Detachment D was able to locate some splendid places to stay, they had bad luck in keeping possession. In Arlon they secured a spectacular mansion in an exclusive residential section of town and quickly got themselves set up. Within one hour they were back on the street. The brass had discovered their magnificent quarters and had usurped it.

Lieutenants James Hanway and Fred Gottlieb pleaded their case to the locals who directed their convoy to St. Donat, an ancient abbey in Clairefontaine, about four miles away. What sounded like a wonderfully romantic place turned out to be a cold, damp, gloomy old building, "more suited for . . . spooks than for the electric spirits of our crew." The only "advantage" was that no one else wanted it. Antennae were hooked from the church steeple, and a high hedgerow provided a place to drape the camouflage nets. After they were in operation in the abbey, the officers coerced their way into Chateau D'Enach, a roomy mansion on the Neufchateau road. This was only ten minutes away and much more comfortable for off-duty hours. Lieutenant Hanway always exhorted the enlisted men to maintain good order of the property they occupied and to remember that they were guests of the nobility, some of whom were still living on the premises.

The surrounding French countryside tempted some of the more adventurous men to explore the nearby caves where the Germans were said to have kept their electrical equipment. Moving slowly into the cold, dark interior, they were immediately alerted by the sound of human voices. Quickly they retreated, rushed back to the chateau, armed themselves with carbines, and returned to capture what turned out to be a little old French woman gathering mushrooms in the underground cavern. Although the men did feel somewhat foolish, they redeemed themselves by collecting a variety of valuable plunder consisting of condensers and resistors that were put to use with American and British equipment.

With Detachment A luxuriating in its "castle" and D stuck in the abbey, Detachment B languished in bleak Jalhay, Belgium, where life in the countryside struggled to go on. For the enlisted men there was little break in the daily routine, but occasionally the superiors were entertained by the local gentry. This was one of the great ironies of wartime — while some bled and died at the front, others enjoyed the local bounty.

Lieutenant Peter White of Detachment B, and some of his fellow officers in Jalhay, were invited to a dinner party at the local baron's home. Feeling that they should dress up for the occasion, the men dug into their footlockers to find awful mildewed shirts. Although their jackets covered the stains, they reeked from the odor. Thinking that this would dissipate by the time they arrived, they wore the smelly garments anyway. As it turned out, their foul gear was the least of the problems at the party.

Upon arrival, they found that the house had been almost completely destroyed by a buzz bomb earlier in the day. But I guess the residents simply got used to the constant unpredictability of life because the baron casually invited them in and the festivities went on as planned. The only change was that dinner was served in the kitchen, one of the few undamaged rooms.

Over an elaborate meal of roasted venison, their help was solicited in discouraging the American soldiers from shooting the baron's deer in the surrounding forest. Perhaps he thought that reverse psychology would work in his choice of entree. It was a very long, drawn-out evening sitting around the table of the manor. White was the only French-speaking guest in attendance, and he recalls putting everyone to sleep with his stories — "a most unusual occurrence," he boasts today with a twinkle. His Commanding Officer, Lieutenant Copp, cheerfully disagrees. "It wasn't an unusual occurrence at all. White would go off on strange little excursions and return to camp with lengthy tales about nothing anyone was ever interested in!"

Always looking for an excuse to make merry, White invited a number of men to rejoice in the birth of his first child, number one of eight. While singing "The Jolly Old Tinker" song, one of his wobbly comrades leaned out the window to share his vocal talents with the uninvited and decided it would be great fun to walk on the glass canopy. He didn't. As soon as he got his second foot out the window and put his bulky weight on the canopy, he found himself sitting on the porch below, covered with sparkling shards. Fortunately, he was unhurt, but when I heard the story later, I remember wondering how the Army would have written up his injury. One soldier had gotten a Purple Heart for trying to make an ashtray out of a German shell, another was sent home for injuries sustained in the "line of duty" when he had sprained his back in a whore house; and the *piéce de résistance* of injuries was yet to come, involving Major Harry Turkel.

Lieutenant Copp also stayed at the little hotel with the other officers and continued blowing electrical circuits with his electric shaver, just as he had done in camp in Normandy; but this time it was a hot plate that he tried to use as a heater. "I was so cold I plugged it in. I just wanted to get warm."

A few days later, the air was riddled with the mournful screech of a dying British Lancaster as it descended to earth. The seemingly endless wail left everyone on edge, and the plane finally found its grave in an enormous crash and explosion. The sobering moment left the men feeling relieved that it had not landed on them, but helpless knowing that the weather and distance prevented them from doing anything until morning. The event touched Lieutenant Copp deeply. He decided to use the occasion to impress upon some of his irresponsible men the seriousness of their duties by sending a number of them to the crash site to bury the remains of the RAF crew — a gruesome, but valuable lesson. What they saw and smelled was forever imprinted upon them. The pilot and co-pilot were burned beyond recognition, another body was in a tree, and the fourth half-buried in the mud. The officer in charge offered the boots of the unburned Brits to the men on burial duty, but no one accepted. Copp said:

> . . . it was a terrible thing. We were the closest outfit to it. I just went up there and stood right by the cockpit of the plane and the pilot and the co-pilot were burned to death. Just ashes. And the sweet smell. I guess that's the way bodies are when they burn. Burned to a crisp.

————◄◦►————

Day-to-day life was tedious and monotonous and compounded by the fact that at this point in the war the men who were stationed in Belgium were restricted to camp to reduce the threat of a German attack. Surrounding towns were off-limits because of snipers and collaborators lurking in the woods and fields. A staff Sergeant was found hanging from a tree near Eupen, and two other GIs were murdered by a little German boy standing on a street corner. This darling little short-panted, alpine-capped child had tossed a bouquet of flowers into their jeep and it exploded. A moment later an enraged MP cut the little boy in two with his Tommy gun. These incidents squelched any desire of the men to venture beyond the confines of their billets. The Jalhay dayroom filled with books and magazines had to suffice.

At night the men would climb the forester's tower located at Baraque Michel, the highest spot in Belgium, to watch the fireworks of battle going on in Aachen 30 miles away, where unbeknownst to them, their Squadron Leader, Major Turkel was picking up some valuable documents in connection with German codes. Aachen was the first large city in Germany captured by us and closer to the front. After the incident, Major Turkel wrote to his children:

> . . . scarcely a roof or floor remained. . . . rubble . . . FLAT. . . . Daddy . . . saw a figure moving in the signal switch house window . . . and began to perspire . . . drew a bead with old Sawtooth . . . and just before he fired . . . discovered it was curtains flapping!

The following week he wrote:

> [In Aachen] Daddy got into bed raw because his pajamas
> were in his bedding roll, but he couldn't sleep because the bed
> was too soft and everything too, too comfortable. Down in the
> street some dog-faces (soldiers that don't belong to Daddy)
> were whooping it up with harmonicas and pretending they were
> hoot owls. . . . Along about midnight Daddy had a bellyful and
> was going to roar to them. . . . Now you must realize that every-
> thing was blacked out and the window was open and it was on
> the 3rd floor. Daddy couldn't put on the light, so he groped his
> way to the window, stumbled over a chair, got tangled in the
> drapes and pitched out of the window. . . . Daddy fell smack on
> his face into the iron railing and got a terrific cut across the
> bridge of his nose. . . . This isn't the first time Daddy has been
> saved by a nose. . . .

It was in Aachen that Captain Bill Shaughnessy was assigned to
"T" Force with Major Turkel and the POW interrogator Major Eric
Warburg, a German refugee in charge of 9th Air Force PWI (Prisoner of
War Interrogation). Their special assignment was to grill German pilots,
and the experience disgusted Shaughnessy.

> I was shocked to see the tactics we used. We would have these
> guys [the enemy] stand up until they were ready to drop and
> then we'd throw cold water at them and they'd stand up again.

When the three officers were interrogating a German captain — a 6-
foot, 2-inch, blond-haired, blue-eyed Aryan — a German-speaking American Tech Sergeant was dressed up as a major and placed behind a desk
where the prisoner was made to stand before him at long intervals, fright-
ened and hungry. Each time he fainted, a pail of water was thrown in his
face, and the pseudo-major would yell, "*Achtung!*" Finally the youth was
taken outside and run up and down a flag pole each time he refused to
answer a question. "What organization are you with?" "How strong are
you?" He never broke. Shaughnessy felt admiration for the young German
as he watched the interrogation, and, finally, with the help of Turkel, carried the youth inside.

———◄o►———

As the war entered December of 1944, the little town of Jalhay in eastern Belgium made plans for an all-out *"fête de Noel."* Dinners were planned for the GIs, and in turn, they organized a Christmas party for the village children, each of whom was to receive a present sent directly from America. Wreaths and garlands decorated the mess hall that had been set up in the inn, and a stately half-trimmed fir tree adorned with colorfully painted dead grenades stood in the corner.

The glistening countryside presented a picture postcard panorama of untouched beauty, masking the horror of war found underneath. The previous month had produced a snowfall of gale intensity. Fir trees bent with their new burden. Deer and rabbit left tracks to mark their territory, showing that life continued as before. It was a crystal fairyland through which daily life tried to push on.

Roads became quagmires, slowing traffic and reducing the high occurrence of accidents, but vehicles finally bowed to the elements and transportation became a thing of the past. When the gripping weather occasionally cleared enough to allow vehicles to move, disgruntled men rode to the mess hall, gulped their food, and rushed back to the transport trucks to avoid being caught in the last run on a cold, dark night in an open truck — a ride from which you seldom thawed out. More often than not they were left huddled in their tents to warm K-rations over little stoves. When the weather did give a moment of respite, liberty runs to hot showers and movies in Verviers boosted the spirits and heightened the men's awareness that they hadn't been forgotten by their superiors. Baths and beers were never enjoyed as much as during the war years. These small luxuries made us all feel very lucky.

During the night, enemy air traffic continued to roar overhead as it had been doing for months, and the area around Jahlay became known as "Buzz Bomb Alley." The men tried to ignore the nerve-shattering sound of Hitler's bombs, a sound that continued incessantly day and night. Postures changed as the screech and silence of the V-1s tore at the men. Shoulders hunched, jaws tightened, and eyes squinted in anticipation of the explosion and the fear of who might become the next target. Afterwards came the unashamed wiping of sweaty foreheads before returning to work.

As Christmas approached, the men began preparing for the festivities in hope that the holiday would be as distracting as Thanksgiving had been. In November, Lieutenant Copp and his officers had cooked for and served the enlisted men. It began with golden roasted turkey stuffed with hearts of celery dressing and all the fixings of mashed potatoes, sweet potatoes, cranberry jelly, and rolls. Although pumpkin pie never materialized, the solders did enjoy candy, fruit, and chocolate cake for dessert. Lieutenants Jim Copp, Jim Goodsell, John Logan, Arnold Shapiro, Selbert Thierfelder, and Peter White happily donned white dish-towel aprons and passed out menus to each man, entitled *Thanksgiving Day in Belgium*. Fun was poked back and forth and dish towels snapped at passing *derrieres*, but no one took advantage of the role reversals. It had been a wonderful break from their dreary routine in a dreary place.

After dinner, the men settled back with warm bellies and outstretched legs, and with glowing cigarettes contemplated where they'd be next year on Thanksgiving Day. Although the best had been made of a bleak situation, and it had been a satisfying time, "Not one man here, who if he had his way, would not rather be in his own home, with his own family, sitting at his own table," reported the camp newspaper. This only increased the men's need to create some excitement as Christmas approached, and the war and the weather hung gloomily in the air.

The officers were billeted at the Hotel de la Couronne, a small inn with a glass canopy that protected the porch below. Here one could sit protected under the awning and enjoy an occasional starry night.

Discipline was paramount at all times, but many of the officers of the squadron were from non-military backgrounds who, although understanding the necessity for following orders, were not interested in the details. Things generally ran smoothly unless someone started drinking. One soldier, an attorney from Oregon, had been transferred to Detachment B in muddy Jalhay as part of his punishment for getting drunk. By the end of the war, his drinking was so bad that it became an embarrassment to everyone, to the point that one day when forced to stand at attention, by the time the flag was down, so was he.

This episode did nothing to curtail his habit. While camped in Thuin, he went off on a drunken spree and phoned his Commanding Officer, Lieutenant Copp. Copp was very annoyed. "Where are you? You have to get back here. You're AWOL."

"Oh, I'm having such a good time."

"Soldier, I put you under arrest."

But in Copp's typical relaxed military fashion he made nothing out of it, never pressing the point, and the man surprisingly returned to camp.

Jalhay at this time was full of excitement. Every day the group's mailman, Dick Almquist, would pick up the unit's mail at the nearest town and deliver it to camp. One afternoon on his way back to Jalhay from Verviers, nine kilometers to the northwest, he spotted some planes rapidly approaching his jeep from the opposite direction. Unconcerned because they were American fighter planes, he continued down the middle of the dirt lane. Suddenly they began firing at him. With a fast turn of the wheel, he bumped off the road and dove for cover, trying to figure out what in the hell was happening. It took weeks before he was able to learn that the Germans had shot down a number of American P-38s and had put them back together with spare parts. They were now using them to cut down unsuspecting GIs.

As winter closed in on our chateau outside of Paris, the Germans no longer showed panic as they regrouped to the north. Their encryption was more stringently controlled, and there were no more wild appeals "in the clear." They were more cautious. We now had to employ more systems to break the code, and as Detachment A's success increased, we became uneasy. Were their messages for real, or were they trying to trick us? This left everyone suspicious of everyone. Perhaps it was a harbinger of what was soon to follow.

The mess hall building at Rue de la Fagne Jalhay, Belgium, November 1944. The men of Detachment B and locals are on the terrace of the inn, used as B's operational base.

Captain Ted Silverstein at Baraque Michel, Belgium, 1944, on the Eupen-Malmédy road.

Below: Fiorella and Detachment D staff at her Chateau La Commanderie, at Fouron St. Pierre, Belgium, November 1944.

COPY

SUPREME HEADQUARTERS
ALLIED EXPEDITIONARY FORCE, (MAIN),
AIR STAFF
Office of the Assistant Chief of Staff A-2

31st October, 1944.

TO: A.C. of S., A-2, S.H.A.E.F. Main.

A report covering the activity of the IXth Air Force Signal
Intelligence Service since D-day until the 26th October has been received,
and provides evidence of the manner in which 'Y' has been used by the IXth
Air Force in the conduct of their tactical battles.

2.   The Squadron, 5 units, has been credited with full responsibility
for the destruction of 272 aircraft, the probable destruction of 39, and
the damage of 32 plus. In addition, they are credited with partial responsibility for the destruction of a further 116 aircraft.

3.   These claims have been made by the Fighter Groups and T.A.C.
concerned and not by the Squadron. Each claim having been completely
investigated and confirmed by the A-2's concerned.

4.   It is safe to say that no results comparable with these have ever
been achieved before by a field 'Y' unit and is due to the enthusiastic
manner in which the IXth Air Force have employed their 'Y' resources. On
many occasions Squadrons have been held at readiness to operate solely on
'Y' information. The results speak for themselves.

(Signed)   G.R. SCOTT FARNIE,

Group Captain,
D/A.C. of S. A-2 (Sig Int).

AEAF/S.16514/Int.

Passed by A.M. Robb to Lt.Gen. Spaatz.

*Par 2: "Full Responsibility" of course refers to the information provided.

True Copy.

(Signed)   G.R. SCOTT FARNIE,

G/Cpt
D/AC of S A-2 (Sig Int)

A TRUE COPY:

W. W. SHAUGHNESSY
Captain, Sig C

British group captain G. R. Scott-Farnie, in charge of training Detachment A in England before
D-Day, reported to SHAEF to congratulate 9th Air Force Signals Intelligence Service (*i.e.*, 3rd
RSM on achieving the best results of any field Intelligence unit (including British) in the Euro-
pean Theater.

Baraque Michel, Belgium, November 1944. Note the forest rangers' tower on the left and the camouflaged D/F van of Detachment B.

The record-breaking Belgian winter of 1944-1945.

-25-   TOP SECRET ULTRA

II   2. The Parachute Landings

The only advance intelligence of the German offensive
received in low-grade air codes was the following
warning of the parachute landings (all times G.M.T.).

1)   16/12. 0415 and 0419 messages intercepted warning
       Flak Units that 90 Ju. 52's and 15 Ju. 88's were
       going from PADERBORN area to area 6° – 6° 30' E.
       to 50° 31' – 50° 45' N. and returning by the
       same route. These messages were cancelled at 0549.

2).   17/12. At 0042 and 0052 similar messages (with T.O.O. = *Time of origin*
       0053 and 0041) were intercepted warning Flak Units
       that 90 Ju. 52's and 15 Ju. 88's were going from
       PADERBORN area to area 6° – 6° 30' E. and 50° 30' –
       50° 45' N. and returning by same route to land at
       0430.   A further message referring to these two
       was intercepted at 0142. "Course North and West".
       The following action was taken:

1)   On 16/12:
(a)   The Operational Watch B.P. phoned Fighter Command,
       Hut 3 (Air and Army), CANTERBURY, and CHEADLE,
       warning CHEADLE that this was not an ordinary
       transport operation. The information was passed to
       Hut 3, D.D.I.3 and D.D.I.4 by teleprinter O.P.I.
       by 0800 hours.
(b)   CHEADLE put the three messages out at 0450, 0455,
       0508 to CANTERBURY for the broadcast to R.A.F. Units
       in FRANCE.
(c)   Operational Watch B.P. put out a considered version
       in G.A.G. teleprints to CANTERBURY for the broadcast
       to R.A.F. Units in FRANCE, to Det. A. for SHAEF A/C
       of S/A-2, CHEADLE D.O., A.I.4.B., A.I.5.B., and MI 14
       ~~Major Owens or Lt. Col. Rhodes's party.~~
       The teleprints were received at CANTERBURY at 1000
       hours (first two messages), 1030 hours third message.

2)   On 17/12 similar action was taken:
       CHEADLE put out the first two messages at 0117 and
       the third at 0224. G.A.G. teleprints were received
       at CANTERBURY at 0155 hours for first two messages
       and 0311 hours for third message.

       It would appear therefore that the cancelled messages
       of 16/12 gave a day's warning of the operation and
       that the messages referring to the operation itself
       were dispatched to Hut 3 and R.A.F. Units in FRANCE
       within half an hour of their receipt here.
       R.A.F. H.Q's. in FRANCE are responsible for passing
       information of interest to the corresponding Army H.Q's.

       It should also be pointed out that all R.A.F. Field
       Units with Groups and the main American Field Unit   = Det "A" 3rd R.S.M(S)
       with the 9th Air Force should have taken and decoded
       the German messages (it is known that 8th Group
       took the messages on 16/12).

Supreme Headquarters' analysis of ULTRA messages received, with comments. This is probably the most telling evidence of SHAEF and other Headquarters not acting on the information.
It is evident that Detachment A *did* get the message.

Captain Jim Copp (Detachment B) with three girls of the Martens family at Chateau Jehanster, Belgium, January 1945.

The label of our champagne "of choice" at Pargny les Reims.

Madame Maltot (proprietress of our "residence") with Lieutenant Mortimer Proctor, at Pargny les Reims, France, February, 1945.

S-E-C-R-E-T

HEADQUARTERS
3rd RADIO SQUADRON MOBILE,(G)
Office of the Commanding Officer.

APO 696, U S Army
12 February 1945

300.6

SUBJECT: Letter of Commendation by CG, Eighth Air Force.

TO : Commanding Officers, All Detachments, 3rd Radio Squadron Mobile(G).

1. The Director of Intelligence and the Director of Communications, Ninth Air Force, desire to add their high commendation to the expressions of appreciation by the Commanding General, Eighth Air Force, and Commanding General, Ninth Air Force.

2. It must be a source of great pride to every member of the Squadron to know that, in our service to the Eighth Air Force alone covering a period of 34 days, the Squadron is exclusively credited with supplying the information which resulted directly in the destruction of 107 enemy aircraft, 7 probables, and 17 damaged.

3. Scores are a convenient, but only approximate method of estimating operational results. They relate only to the offensive use of "Y". The defensive use of "Y" is equally important, but it will never be known how many American aircraft and crews were saved by our timely warning, or, in connection with our service to the various Tactical Air Commands, how many American ground troops were protected owing to the frustration of German air attacks.

4. The operational successes of the 3rd Radio Squadron flow in part from the high efficiency of its individual members, but principally because the intercept, D/F, communications, and intelligence sections within each detachment form a team; because the various R/T detachments with the W/T detachment together form a team; because the Squadron itself working with fighter controllers and Staff "Y" officers form a team.

5. This teamwork will continue until the last aircraft ceases to fly under Nazi markings.

6. The contents of the basic communication and indorsements are not to be posted but will be read to members of your command at formation under appropriate security precautions. It would be appreciated if you would indicate to each member of the Squadron present the pride and affection felt toward him by the Commanding Officer, 3rd Radio Squadron Mobile.

/S/ HARRY R. TURKEL
/T/ HARRY R. TURKEL
Lt. Col, Air Corps
Commanding

S-E-C-R-E-T
-1-

Colonel Turkel's letter to all men of the 3rd RSM, adding his appreciation to General Doolittle's commendation.

Part of Detachment A's group photo, March 1945, at Pargny les Reims. The officers are the first six men seated on left of lowest row: Lieutenants Proctor, Ogren, and Davidson; Captain Brinson; Lieutenants Cox and Small.

Balance of Detachment A group photo, March 1945, at Pargny les Reims.

Major Ted Silverstein's sketch of a happy, hectic Paris on V-E Day, May 8, 1945.

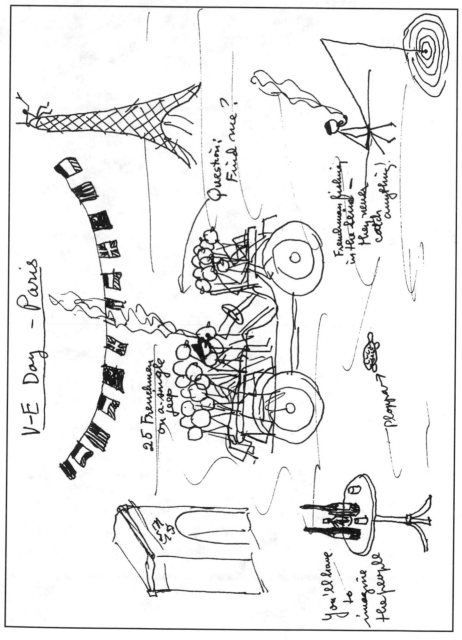

Liege, Belgium, rejoices in the return of all its victims of German barbarism, May 1945.

This inaction and indecisiveness by U.S. Headquarters
. . . left the Allies completely unprepared for the enormous
onslaught . . . and the beginning of the Bulge.

Chapter Thirteen

The Bulge and the Blunder

T HE EERIE STILLNESS that engulfed the forward area of the war zone in Belgium caused it to be known as the "ghost front." Tension increased daily, but in this calm no one knew why. Only the high-ranking Allied officers privy to secret information knew that the Germans were preparing an attack. Maybe the men sensed their concern. The Germans, having tried the same plan two times in the beginning of the 20th century, first through Belgium in 1914 and later through the Netherlands and the Ardennes in 1940 with Operation Case Yellow, were now going to try again to reach their goal through the Ardennes Forest, in easternmost Belgium. They were stubborn and they were savage.

As the German infantry was planning its offensive, Lieutenant Colonel Friedrich August Freiherr von der Heydte was given one week to put together a parachute strike force to hook up with the foot soldiers. To his unit were sent the "sad sacks," the physical and mental misfits, from Commanders wishing to dump their problem men. After the war he said:

> I quickly replaced the men whose fighting spirit appeared lowest with trustworthy volunteers from the school units, thereby including a number of men with no previous experience. They would jump for the first time on the night of 16-17 December. From what I could learn, these men stood the test amazingly well, proving that special training is not as essential as a stout heart and a dexterous body that has been trained by sports.

On December 8, 1944, von der Heydte's men were vaccinated against tetanus, gangrene, and typhoid and their underwear impregnated with louse repellent. Six days later they were sent to a military camp to await the beginning of Operation Auk — code name for his mission in the Battle of the Bulge — and for orders to jump behind Allied lines in Belgium. Arriving at 2 a.m., they found that no instructions had been given for their billeting. Von der Heydte was furious. His 1,200 German paratroopers had no place to sleep or even rest!

Because the unit was so poorly trained, he attempted to voice his overall objections to the mission, but was rudely dismissed by a drunken General der Flieger Beppo Schmidt. Appealing to a higher court, Field Marshal Walter Model, involved in the decision-making, asked von der Heydte if he gave the parachute drop a ten percent chance of success. When he answered "yes," Model told him to proceed because it was

> the last remaining hope to conclude the war favorably. If the most [is] not made of that ten percent chance, Germany [will] be faced with certain defeat.

In a last-ditch effort to prepare his men, von der Heydte asked General Sepp Dietrich his opinion about the enemy forces, but Dietrich was uncooperative:

> I am not a prophet. You will learn earlier than later what
> forces the Americans will employ against you. Besides, behind
> their lines there are only Jewish hoodlums and bank managers.

Von der Heydte gritted his teeth. He was not a Nazi. He was from an
aristocratic Catholic family, and had studied law and served as an assistant
professor of jurisprudence in Berlin. During that time he had banished
himself from the Third Reich when authorities ousted a Jewish professor
from the university.

Holding his temper with Dietrich, he asked for carrier pigeons in case
of communication equipment failure.

"I am not running a zoo," snapped the General.

This was only the beginning of the fiasco. Against all odds, Lieutenant
Colonel von der Heydte followed orders.

The next night the planes would travel the final 50 kilometers with only
wing lights for illumination. On the back of each paratrooper would be a
parachute packed by a foreign slave laborer, having arrived too late for
inspection and repacking, a standard procedure to prevent sabotage.

On December 15, 1944, the Allies' ULTRA code breakers decrypted
the following message sent from Luftwaffe Command Center to
Wehrkreis VI:

> Senne 1 (Paderborn Airport) prescribed as take-off airfield
> for a unit connected with Transport Command. Nearby airfields
> listed as intermediate fuelling-points.

At this stage in the war the Germans were avoiding radio transmissions
because they suspected that we were breaking their messages, although
they didn't know how. Anything of a highly secretive nature was delivered
either by hand or by telephone over secured lines. Because of their grad-
ual increased radio silence and the routine nature of our work, it was
important to remain alert and not be lulled into complacency by the repet-
itiveness. German pilots seldom said anything of interest when they were
in the air, and the content of their messages was often predictable, so it
was easy to let boredom take over. Our challenge was to catch the important ones and figure out what they meant. We sat waiting.

On December 16th, out of the silence, our radios came alive. The staccato bark of the German radio operator filled the air waves of Detachment

A still camped at Chateau Beaumont near Paris. We intercepted identical ELGAR messages at 0415 and 0419. (ELGAR was the German code, commonly used for contacting their anti-aircraft units.) But these messages didn't make sense. Were they trying to fool us with another "spoof" message? During the invasion of Normandy we had unsuccessfully struggled with the transmission, "Periscope up," and now 3rd RSM had another puzzling communication, and no clue as to what it meant. It was a red flag — but one we couldn't figure out.

The second message that was sent only four minutes after the first confirmed the number 90. We initially thought that this might be an error in encryption. Ninety transport planes moving simultaneously? Very strange.

Later we learned that von der Heydte was notifying his anti-aircraft batteries not to fire at a certain time that night. When we broke his message, we had more questions to answer. Why was he ordering this, and perhaps more importantly, why was the message repeated? It seemed clear to us that the Germans wanted to move their own aircraft into position during this time, but why was the message sent again? Never in our whole code-breaking experience had a message been repeated. Was he attempting to mislead us?

The Unit History of A later recorded:

> 16/12 [at] 0415 and 0419 messages intercepted warning Flak Units that 90 Ju. 52's and 15 Ju. 88's were going from Paderborn area to area 6°-6°30' E. to 50°31'-50°45' N. and returning by the same route.

Rarely had that many transport planes been sent together. And 15 fighter bombers? What was going on? We notified SHAEF, 9th Air Force, and all appropriate detachments. The brains of Detachment A, Lieutenants Proctor and Davidson, decided that so many transports into Allied airspace signified only one thing: a paratroop drop. The officers dispatched the decoded message to 9th AF Headquarters in Luxembourg City, to IX TAC at Verviers, and to SHAEF in Versailles with the admonition, *"Number of transports repeated in cipher can only indicate paratroop drop."* The Headquarters merely acknowledged:

QRV [Message received.]

While we were puzzling over the German transmissions, we received a message in the clear 30 minutes later at 0549, canceling the others. It turned out that these interceptions would be some of the first German orders of the Battle of the Bulge.

————————◄○►————————

Unable to get trucks to transfer the men from the barracks to the planes because no fuel had been authorized, the Luftwaffe's mission had to be aborted. Von der Heydte was livid. He had been in the war since the beginning. He had captured a major airfield in Holland, had earned the Collar of Knight of the Iron Cross for commanding a paratroop battalion in the Battle of Crete, and had gained fame by commanding the parachute regiment that had delayed the Americans from breaking through at Carentan. Now he was immobilized in camp because he couldn't get any trucks or pilots!

As a result of the confusion and inability of getting his outfit transported to the airport, von der Heydte had sent a frenzied last-minute message canceling the mission.

While this was going on, SHAEF was trying to evaluate the significance of Detachment A's break, but didn't think that the German army had enough strength to take the offensive. Underestimating Jerry's ability, General Eisenhower continued his social engagements of a wedding reception and a few rubbers of Bridge. Major General Everett Hughes from SHAEF reported:

> Brad [Omar Bradley] says Germans have started a big counterattack towards [General] Hodges. Very calm about it. Seemed routine from his lack of emphasis.

This inaction and indecisiveness by U.S. Headquarters was interpreted by my unit as a somewhat lackadaisical attitude regarding the value of our information, and left the Allies completely unprepared for the enormous onslaught along the entire 80-mile Belgian-Luxembourg front and the beginning of the Bulge.

The following day, the puzzle became even more baffling for Detachment A. The message that had been sent the previous day was again transmitted.

———————◄O►———————

Lieutenant Colonel von der Heydte was finally able to move his troops to Senne 1 — one of two airfields there, but he still faced obstacles. For some unknown reason, the Commander of Wehrkreis VI had done everything in his power to prevent the airport in his sector from being used for this action, and General Rundstedt, Commander in Chief of the Battle of the Bulge, had to step in and give emphatic orders to the contrary. Scheduled to rendezvous behind enemy lines, von der Heydte was desperate. He again attempted to notify German anti-aircraft units to withhold their fire.

German paratroopers finally boarded the aircraft and received the weather report indicating a wind velocity of six meters per second above the landing zone in the Eupen-Malmédy area, the highest wind velocity permissible for a night drop into a wooded location. When they jumped, the wind speed was actually 17 meters per second, triple the acceptable limit. "Presuming a higher wind velocity above the landing area, I would have refused to jump," said von der Heydte. Too late to retreat, he accepted that his superiors had lied to ensure that the mission would not be aborted. To make matters worse, the jump masters gave orders solely based on their estimates of the necessary clock time involved in the jump, rather than taking into account observations of the landing area which might affect that time. The jump, therefore, was only partially successful; a mere one-third of the planes had dropped their human cargo in the right place. Some men landed more than 50 miles from the target.

The German paratroopers were whipsawed by the high wind and crashed into trees or the ground, breaking arms and legs and backs. All this was exacerbated by the fact that many of the German gun batteries didn't get the message to withhold their fire and shot at their own planes, destroying a number of them. The paratroopers didn't have a chance with both Germans and Americans shooting at them simultaneously.

As was the custom, the leader — Lieutenant Colonel von der Heydte — jumped first. With his arm in a sling from a previous injury, he landed on target, but in a tree that broke the wounded arm. This second injury became infected and von der Heydte developed pneumonia, which ultimately led to his eventual surrender. Totally isolated from his troops after his jump, he managed to rendezvous later with only 25 of his original 1,200 men. The casualty numbers increased dismally, and from his small group von der Heydte dispatched reconnaissance patrols. They were to

avoid all contact with the enemy unless they were able to capture solo
message-bearers. Thirty-six Americans were caught! The information the
Germans procured from these prisoners was a major success, but von der
Heydte could do nothing with it:

> If only I had been able to transmit it. Unfortunately because
> of the high wind velocity during the airdrop, every radio set had
> been lost, and I had not been given any carrier pigeons.

He counted his men — only 300 of the original 1,200 had landed in a location that enabled them to regroup. Subsequently, a couple days later, when
he finally had decided the mission was a failure, he released his prisoners.

The U.S. Army document, declassified and released to the National
Archives in August 1996, evaluated the causes of the Allied Intelligence
failure prior to the German attack:

> It would appear therefore that the canceled messages of
> 16/12 gave a day's warning of the operation and that the mes-
> sages referring to the operation itself were dispatched to Hut 3
> and R.A.F. Units in FRANCE within half an hour of their
> receipt here. . . . and the American Field Unit (Detachment A,
> 3rd RSM) with the 9th Air Force should have taken and de-
> coded the German messages.

Well, we *did* decode the messages, but it didn't seem like anyone was
listening.

Meanwhile, Captain Silverstein, still waiting with Detachment B at
Jalhay, was convinced that something was about to blow. He called IX
TAC Headquarters at Verviers. Not satisfied with their response, he
jumped into his jeep and went to see if anything was happening. Search-
lights were combing the sky and the reflection off the clouds was so bright
that you could read a newspaper at 3 a.m. First Army had figured out the
German flight path, and our AA guns were taking their toll.

Returning to Detachment B, Silverstein waited. During the coldest winter in 25 years, the GIs slept, secure that no action would take place this
freezing night. Because of the decoded messages received from Detachment A, Silverstein knew there would be a paratroop drop, but he didn't
know where or when. As a non-combat officer, he never suspected that he

would have Germans jumping almost over his head putting him in the center of the action!

Toward early morning, a German paratrooper dropped away from the roar of the Ju.52's engines and drifted into the eerie stillness and ghostly desolation of cold silence. The smooth, snowy wasteland was devoid of habitation, its serene crystal beauty glistening in all directions. It was a "No Man's Land." The end of the world. Yet, amidst this solitude he knew that he was not alone. Carefully he disengaged his lifeline. He moved forward. Every slow, laborious crunch of his boot upon the crust brought fear of enemy reprisal. As he moved past the foe, he knew that his goal was up the road, not here. Ignoring the sleeping Americans, he pushed onward, aware that complete secrecy was paramount.

During the night, 90 Ju.52s had flown overhead and more than 1,000 paratroopers had dropped from the sky. Not one was detected. How was this possible? We had been waiting for something to happen.

Dawn brought a jarring shock. As the men on night duty from Detachment B were returning from their assignment — their "trick" — at Baraque Michel, they peered into the distance and slowly recognized the lifeless forms of the parachutes.

Gathering one up for evidence, Kurt Tannenwald, Al Gruber, and a few others rushed back to Headquarters excitedly reporting what they had seen. Stunned, Silverstein's first thought was that his "cloak of invisibility" had been removed, adding "This is my worst nightmare. If they're after us, we can't risk capture."

Silverstein didn't know if the Germans had landed there by accident or by design, but he did know that his Intelligence unit could not risk being found, under any circumstance. Jerry and GI alike understood the need for secrecy and had tried to remain invisible to each other. Silverstein feared that his cover was blown and his location discovered, but he had no way of confirming it. If this was so, why had his men been left unharmed? It was a mystery.

He called IX TAC at Verviers for instructions. Bewildered and alarmed, those at Headquarters were indecisive. After much persistence on his part for a decision, Silverstein was finally told to just stay put.

At this same time, Detachment B's Staff Sergeant Bob Siefert had been sent from Jalhay, to Baraque Michel, six miles southeast of Jalhay, on the main road from Eupen to Malmédy, to pick up the daily logs. On his way he noticed several empty parachutes hanging from the trees. He later noted:

> . . . it didn't dawn on me at the time as to what had happened until I got to Baraque Michel. One man [American] stood guard outside the entrance which was but a few feet off the road, and four or five German paratroopers walked past. . . . He [the guard] stood very still and never challenged them.

In the shadows, Siefert watched. Both sides seemed to want to make the other disappear by the simple act of ignoring one another. The American knew that if he moved, he would be killed. The Germans knew that if gunfire was heard, it would blow their cover and alert the Americans that their line had been infiltrated; so they simply marched on.

When Siefert got back to camp, he told his unbelievable story to Captain Silverstein, a story that only added to his CO's discomfiture. It was an unusual moment in the war. Both sides knew it was in its death throes, and they simply wanted to survive.

While Silverstein had impatiently waited for Headquarters to make its decision, he had ordered Lieutenant Peter White to investigate the surrounding area. Jumping into the nearest jeep, White drove through the parachute-littered fields and into the forest where he found an American infantry unit wandering around. The Sergeant in charge asked White to lead the way — take charge of them — and his men would follow.

> I felt that I couldn't refuse. I came from a long line of soldiers and generals; my grandfather was on Pershing's staff, my

father was Wilson's naval aide, there were four or five Revolutionary generals and a Secretary of War in my background, so I thought that if he tells me to command I must do it. . . . I thought up this idiot cops and robbers plan [to give us a mission out there], and we went into the woods and captured a Belgian professor and three students out for a walk.

At this point White decided that the Sergeant should have been the leader and suggested that they all get the hell out of there. He immediately returned to Jalhay and reported his "capture" of the locals.

———◄o►———

Silverstein and Copp waited impatiently for orders. They knew that their location was no longer secure and that to remain put them in jeopardy of being surrounded and captured, but Headquarters was either unable or unwilling to make a decision.

The silence and inactivity became unbearable, and thus Silverstein contacted Headquarters again. The people there were so rattled that no one would give an order. Worried, Silverstein returned to camp. "If [the Germans] had spotted us then it was just damn right that we should get the hell out of there in a hurry," he said. Finally, Silverstein and Copp gave the command to move out. "We just made up our own orders," White said. That was true, but not as cavalier as it may sound. Silverstein had standing orders that if the Germans started attacking, he was to get out immediately. Now he did.

Suddenly the full force of the German attack began, and everything became a beehive of activity. The roar of tanks and planes was constant, and roads of the Ardennes Forest were jammed with people and vehicles going in all directions. Eisenhower and Montgomery were not surprised by the attack, only by the strength of it. Their personal conflicts with each other added to the confusion, resulting in Headquarters looking like a disturbed anthill. One officer panicked and tried to crank a crankless jeep, while others were jumping into any vehicle moving along the body-littered roads. No one seemed to know what was happening or what to do.

Around Jalhay, German planes flew at tree-top level, and by morning Jerry was nearing Malmédy, headed toward Verviers, threatening our Direction Finding station some nine miles away at Baraque Michel. The men on duty there were quickly ordered to evacuate and retreat. In two short hours the gigantic feat of moving all equipment and personnel in precise order was accomplished.

Returning to Jalhay, they found the tiny village in bedlam. American tanks were rumbling through the streets as German flares lighted the sky. Sleep became impossible. Men crowded head to foot wherever they could throw their gear, collapsing from exhaustion. The kitchen served stragglers around the clock as they staggered in, almost numb to their hunger and fatigue. Soon it became clear that our entire Army was falling back, but Headquarters still remained silent.

In Detachment B, Lieutenant Selbert Thierfelder informed Copp that the civilians in the village wanted to be armed so that they could help fight the Germans, and they had requested a meeting to discuss it. Copp later noted,

> I consented [to the meeting], but immediately discovered that the men were trigger-happy and therefore [I] refused to supply weapons. I realized that they would shoot anyone, and it would become a blood bath.

Against the advice of most of his top generals, Hitler executed his self-devised attack — what would be called the Battle of the Bulge or the Ardennes Offensive — to cut the Allied forces in two and separate the Eupen-Malmédy sector from the south, with Panzer divisions and infantry led by Field Marshal Gerd von Rundstedt. In dense fog, driving rain, and penetrating cold, Generals Sepp Dietrich, Hasso von Manteuffel, and Ernst Brandenberger hit with the impact of 24 divisions, 14 infantry, and 10 armored. At 5 a.m. on December 16th, the Germans draped "the fog of war" about them like a mantle and moved endless columns of tanks, artillery, and infantry into Belgium under the cover of darkness over snow-covered arterial roads. Unseen, at dawn they deployed with all their terrible grim gear, hoping to connect with their paratroopers.

When the rumble of tanks, and the roar of trucks was heard, we initially refused to give credence to the possibility that the Germans were on the move. The earlier use of phonograph records to create the sounds of vehicles led us to believe that what we were hearing was fake. The idea that a major assault would occur by such a weakened army was summarily dismissed. And thus, when the Germans hit, the Americans were outnumbered ten to one, and unable to communicate with one another because of the distance between foxholes.

After the first day, only one American company Commander could be found. Darkness set in and fear increased. Semi-organized confusion reigned. No one had sufficient ammunition, and the lack of winter gear made the weather as deadly an enemy as the Germans. The only warmth available was distilled alcohol or a body to lean against, alive or barely dead.

Death was at random. Bullets hit soldiers, tossing them into the air, whipping them around, and splattering blood and flesh on those near. The "rag men," those wounded, patched up, and sent immediately back into action, knew no future. They became afraid of everything. As new recruits were fed into the meat grinder of battle to replace the fallen, they were told, "Most of you are not coming back. You may as well get used to it." Two thousand a day were killed, many on their first day of battle.

The Battle of the Bulge was one of the biggest, most stunning, and most confused battles of World War II. The front line became a broken puzzle as Germans and Allies alternated control of neighboring towns. Both sides captured, liberated, and recaptured the same ground as power flip-flopped back and forth between enemies.

Germany's initial attack had come as a great surprise and achieved astonishing success. With newly instilled confidence, they demanded surrender. American Brigadier General Anthony McAuliffe's answer was simply, "Nuts."

But Jerry's success was short-lived, as British General Bernard Montgomery, and American Generals Omar Bradley and George Patton squeezed and destroyed — Montgomery and Bradley from the north and west, Patton from the south. The battle ended a month later, almost where it had begun. Germany's resources were by then so depleted that resistance to the fast-moving Russians from the east was impossible.

Over one million men fought in the Bulge. Eight thousand American soldiers were killed, 48,000 wounded, and 20,000 were captured or missing. Because of the tremendous loss of lives, it was considered a Pyrrhic victory. It was also the last German gasp of the war.

General Eisenhower later admitted that we were caught by surprise, but added that the attack brought the Germans out of their Siegfried Line defenses and into the open where we were able to destroy them. The Bulge marked the beginning of the last 100 days of the 1,000-year Third Reich.

*. . . During wartime pressures, personalities and battle
fatique sometimes skewed priorities and judgment. . . .
Even the judgment of the brilliant General Vandenberg
. . . was suspect when he ordered one of the **Westa Eins**
planes shot down. . . .*

Chapter Fourteen

Maneuvers, Mistakes, and Mayhem

ORTUNATELY THE WEATHER earlier in December 1944, during the beginning of the Bulge, had been more hospitable to radio reception. This had enabled Detachment A to receive and break important messages that resulted in significant German losses. Now, late in the month, dense fog enveloped the Parisian countryside, reducing visibility to zero, inhibiting all air operation, and significantly interfering with our role as Intelligence liaison to 9th Air Force Headquarters and 3rd RSM's detachments. But our Wehrmacht counterparts were in the same situation, since both radio and air traffic were virtually nil.

Even though the fog caused our code-breaking responsibilities to decrease, we were not unemployed. My "off duty" time was spent patrolling the area around Chateau Beaumont in the bitter cold. With carbine in hand, I performed four-hour shifts searching for *Fallschirmjaeger* — paratroopers — and then tried to thaw out my body the rest of the night. For nine days conditions remained unchanged — fog, rain, snow, grounded aircraft.

Although it had been a time of frustration, it had also been a time of accomplishment with our December 16th interception of the German plan for the paratrooper drop. The 3rd RSM Unit History recorded that accomplishment with three succinct sentences:

> A message was intercepted which reported the movement of a number of transport planes, suggesting an airborne operation. This was confirmed later by a report that paratroops had been dropped in this sector. Ample warning was given of this operation, and 19 planes were destroyed.

But the circumstances surrounding that interception remain a "sore point" with the men of Detachment A. Detachment A *had* sent on the decrypted message to all relevant units of 3rd RSM, warning of an impending enemy drop. Detachment B *had* reported finding empty parachutes. And it was my impression that Detachment A *had* "kraced" the message and *had* sent it on to SHAEF, 9th Air Force, and the other higher Headquarters. Yet none of this succeeded in jarring SHAEF into action. For those directly involved, the lack of responsiveness was frustrating and frightening.

There appears to be considerable discrepancy between fact and fiction. Memory and "matter" do not always agree. SHAEF's after-battle critique, part of the U.S. Army document declassified August 1996, states:

> This order [Detachment A's interception] of 16/12 was clearly the final starting gun. But it was received too late for warning.

According to Major Silverstein and Captain Copp, however, as well as Detachment A, there was *plenty of warning*, but it was unheeded.

In retrospect, we can conjecture why Detachment A was ignored; but at the time, it was difficult to understand. Perhaps the problem simply lay in the difference between the types of codes the Germans had used and the significance the U.S. Army gave to them.

We, with 3rd RSM, handled the "low-grade" Intelligence codes — commonly the musical instrument codes, such as TRUMPET and OBOE, or the composer codes like ELGAR, BEETHOVEN, and SHUBERT. Anything involving the magnitude of the Battle of the Bulge would usually be transmitted in *utmost secrecy* using "high-grade" code — what was called ULTRA. And this may have led to the assumption by Headquarters that the messages we had intercepted were not of great importance. SHAEF's declassified document does admonish the participants in the fiasco:

> There is a risk of relying too much on Source [ULTRA]. His very successes in the past constitute a danger. . . . The evidence . . . was passed in its abundance to those responsible. But in its very abundance, in its very authenticity, lie dangers. . . . Source gave all he knew: but he does not always know everything. . . .

And, thus, 3rd RSM's Y Intelligence, with its low-grade codes, continued to live in the shadow of ULTRA. The declassified SHAEF document offered another possible explanation for Headquarters' lack of action:

> . . . Here does exist a besetting tendency in Intelligence . . . the tendency to become too wedded to one view of enemy intentions. It had grown to be generally believed that the Germans would not counter-attack, head-on . . . [U]nless Intelligence is perpetually ready to entertain all the alternatives, it sees only the evidence that favours the chosen view.

Beginning in October 1944, the evidence provided by ULTRA gave SHAEF ample reason to suspect that the German Air Force was preparing to bring the bulk of its combat planes onto its airfields in western Germany. We understood that this action was in support of their Army. By early November, German fighter units were ordered to send advanced detachments to the west. This began to happen later that month, and in an undated, TOP SECRET ULTRA document, it was recorded:

> . . . Generals Bradley and Strong both [are] known to have
> agreed several times in December that attack in Ardennes was
> [in] the cards. . . . Evidence that the blow was imminent
> appeared from about December 4; possible evidence of its tim-
> ing and duration was also available. . . . Evidence of precise
> point of attack was never clear.

At the same time, there were rumors afloat of a plot to infiltrate our lines with German paratroopers. And interestingly, because their uniforms looked similar to British battle dress, the Germans were concerned that they might be captured and executed, for wearing the British uniform — the uniform of the enemy — a violation of the Hague Convention.

The threat of impostors had plagued us throughout the war. One tip-off that helped to identify the enemy was that the German-Germans spoke flawless English — the German-Americans did not. There were many refugees in our unit with thick German accents, men like Kurt Tannen-wald, who had been selected for their language skills. And as the threat of mistaken identity increased, so did the harassment; Tannenwald continued to be an easy target for the MPs who used questions about baseball and movie stars to establish whether soldiers were really from the U.S. This drove him crazy because he had absolutely no interest or knowledge in either of these popular American pastimes.

In addition to accents, anyone in a jeep was suspect. The Germans had captured and airlifted several of the vehicles into the area to add credibil-ity to their disguise. Even Silverstein was singled out. With his jeep and British accent, he got a double whammy.

This continuing threat from impersonators motivated the U.S. Army into replacing all white MPs with blacks, since there was no way they could be mistaken for Germans. Being immediately identifiable, they could patrol the streets at night without problems. If you were a white man walking the streets you might get arrested or possibly shot.

On December 16th, the night of the German paratroop drop, some unsuspecting officers from First Army Headquarters at Spa went deer hunting in the woods and bagged a German paratrooper hanging from a tree. While they were bringing him back for interrogation, the Belgian forester who had been hired to guide the officers on the hunt, went over the mountain to warn the civilians. Suddenly he found himself surrounded by men from a black Engineering unit. No one was able to speak French, and with suspicions running high, he was arrested. The poor forester spent the night in jail for breaking curfew, and the rest of the Engineering unit never found out about the paratroopers until they ran into them walking down the road the next day in broad daylight. Because the German uniforms looked so much like the British uniforms, the locals initially had mistaken the paratroopers for Englishmen, happily waved "Hi," and threw cigarettes in a gesture of friendship. But as soon as the paratroopers tried to communicate, the Americans realized their mistake and took prisoners.

◄◦►

On December 20, 1944, Detachment A played host to a council of Y units in Europe. At Chateau Beaumont, officers from the British 382nd Wireless unit, plus American Detachments A, C, and E, were present. British Wing Commander Rowley Scott-Farnie headed the meeting assisted by Flight Officer Jones and Squadron Leader Waters, all from SHAEF. A plan was proposed to eliminate QRM (static) on channel and operational frequencies, and information was released concerning a new cipher machine — ENIGMA. According to Lieutenant Proctor's diary, the meeting went very well:

> The American units were not all represented by reason of the new German offensive. Detachments B and D were pinned down and busy. Lts. Heinrich and Furth of Det. C were here, as were two officers from the orphan E. It was a supremely successful meeting, chiefly because Lt. Col. Turkel was not present, he too was tied down in Luxembourg, to everyone's relief. . . .

Turkel had been demanding of his men lately, but what Proctor and the men didn't know was the reason, the real cause of his absence.

ELGAR, the code we had been working with, was a major source of important information about German anti-aircraft batteries. With the discovery that a German offensive was planned, Turkel knew that the information gleaned from messages in this code had become even more critical. And thus, when communication broke down, he blew his cool and snapped at those responsible. Proctor's diary reads:

Yesterday the most awful "flap" arose over Elgar. It all began
when we missed one on the day before; reception had been
stinking and the headsets . . . suddenly went bad and produced
only QRM (static). Well, Lt. Small had the misfortune to tell
Fetter about it up in Luxembourg and Fetter told Col. Turkel.
Then it came fast. Turkel went to Col. Cody, threatened to move
the unit if they couldn't pick it up, and told Fetter he could have
as many men as he wanted to cover the frequency. All this, too,
without bothering to call back here and find out that the difficulty had arisen from a simple technical failure. He simply went
out of his mind. For two months now we have been giving him
this stuff without a flaw — but he didn't think of that.

As Lieutenant Proctor was cooling his heels and his temper, Colonel
Turkel was becoming more annoyed by little things. One of the officers,
he complained,

> gravels me by eating in the continental manner. It gripes me
> terribly to see any one wearing the uniform of an officer in the
> U.S. Army shoveling away with the fork upside down in the left
> hand!

Pressure was coming from all sides for everyone, and those without full
knowledge of the consequences weren't able to understand the significance of a "lost" ELGAR message at this point in the war. It was simply
an issue of "need to know." Colonel Turkel *needed* to know; the subordinates didn't. The other thing they didn't need to know was the real reason
behind Turkel's absence from the Y conference.

Harry Turkel, our squadron leader, who was constantly moving from
detachment to detachment and incident to incident, was not fully involved
in the action at the time of the Bulge due to an embarrassing injury. Being
repeatedly exposed to enemy fire, he never anticipated that his war wound
would come from a fellow officer. It wasn't until after the war, in 1955, on
a trip back to Jalhay, Belgium, that he finally explained the circumstances
to his wife:

> Look, Marge, here's how it happened. [In mid-November] I
> had just come back from Maastricht where it had been pretty

bad, and we had been shelled on the way. I was cold and tired
out, and it was six o'clock. I sat down here [in the mess hall].
. . . Silverstein sat down on my left and showed me a captured
Belgian pistol he had been putting together. "This is how it
works," he said and pulled back the sear on top of the barrel
[and it fired]. The bullet hit my wrist, passed through into my
groin [and through my testicle]. . . . I stood up and said to
Silverstein, "Why you damned fool," and turned and walked
away. . . . I staggered a few steps and . . . collapsed at the foot
of the stairs.

After Turkel had recovered, he related this story to 9th Air Force Radar
Officer Colonel Jerry Stover. "This is really embarrassing. Where am I
going to tell people I was wounded?" Stover's solution was simple: "Tell
them you were wounded in Belgium."

During recovery, Lieutenant Copp took dictation for a letter to
Turkel's children. The incident was described with humor and light-
heartedness:

Dear Children,
     . . . the measly little bullet went through Daddy's forearm
(left) very courteously not touching either arteries or nerves and
then into his left groin, just piercing the bladder. Daddy felt as
though someone kicked him and then spilled hot soup over him.
Daddy walked off in a very high dudgeon and about 12 steps
later it hit him like a ton of bricks. I regret to inform you that
your Father took no further interest in the war because he
passed out cold . . . he shook so hard that if you had hooked up
a butter paddle to him, you could have made butter out of
cream.
     . . . Sgt. Rozansky, the cook . . . began to pray, but Daddy was
very happy floating on clouds what with all the dope. . . .
     Within an hour a heated ambulance was driven up, which
was welcome, because Daddy, the old sap, was getting pretty
soggy. . . .
     [At] 77th Evacuation Hospital . . . the litter bearers took
Daddy out very gently and laid him . . . in a low and drafty cor-
ridor . . . which Daddy used to shoot his cookies. . . . Daddy

wasn't really sick understand, but he was annoyed with all the foolish questions, like "What state were you born in?" and "How much is 1906 plus 38 divided by years of service? . . . . They took him to the operating room. "Oh, what a beautifully clean shot," said the first doctor looking at Daddy's left forearm. "What a fine wound," said a second. "How perfect," murmured a third. Daddy perked up and felt quite proud. Then they looked at his left groin. "How interesting," said the first. "Extraordinary," said the second. "H-m-m," said the third. The nurses peeked over, and shook their heads. My spirits dropped.

> Love and kisses to you and mama from
> your Perforated Papa.

In his next letter he wrote:

> Daddy, that original guy, instead of having to go to the plumbing, had the plumbing hooked up to him . . . but Daddy insisted on changing his own bandages. Daddy became a ward boy and brought ducks to the poor infantry boys who were in casts. "Ducks" are enamel [urinal] containers that just look like ducks.

Later, Lieutenant Colonel Turkel, received a medal for his war efforts in Belgium, and he wrote:

> The General clapped his hands and gave Daddy a red piece of ribbon to wear on his chest and a yellow wreath on his arm. . . . Daddy will give you the red ribbons but you needn't be proud of them because they are getting to be like noses — everybody has one.

I often wondered if a Purple Heart would have been appropriate for a wound to that part of the anatomy!

Recognition was valuable, but not always as significant as it seemed. Turkel's evaluation of his award was shared by Captain Gottlieb who told me after the war that he had received two bronze stars — the first for his landing in Normandy, and,

I think the way this came about was that the second one was handed out en masse. Each outfit [of] the 9th Air Force got fifty of them, and the Commanding Officer would decide who would get what.

That didn't mean that the recipients weren't proud of them, only that they understood the circumstances. Perhaps John O'Hara's description of his Presidential Unit Citation insignia on his now snug Eisenhower jacket says it all. "It looks just like a toilet seat. And the jacket shrunk after fifty years of hanging in the closet!" I didn't tell him that mine hadn't.

———◄o►———

Fortunately Colonel Turkel recovered from his wound, but the accidental shooting left Captain Silverstein badly shaken. Lieutenant White, who was present at the debacle recounted how extraordinarily chivalrous Turkel was about the whole thing. He never again mentioned the incident to Silverstein.

At about this time, Silverstein's promotion to Major came through, and while he was awaiting further assignment, Copp — now a Captain — took charge and became the "Old Man" of Detachment B. Silverstein had been an exemplary officer and Commander of B, frequently not stopping to eat or sleep as he pushed himself around the clock, but now stress and fatigue were beginning to show. He had pushed himself beyond endurance, and like Colonel Turkel, had become very demanding.

While in Thuin during the Bulge, he was inspecting Detachment B's vehicles. They were a bunch of shabby, old, olive-drab British trucks that didn't come up to military standards of appearance. "Jim. Get this outfit looking better. Get it looking better," he demanded as he left for the local "castle." Copp put Sergeant Taylor in charge and he got all the vehicles in great condition. Each received a new coat of drab and flawless, white, five-pointed stars in perfect circles painted on their sides. They looked terrific. But instead of acknowledging the accomplishment, Silverstein simply overlooked it and made another demand. Captain Copp blew. Over the phone he said, "Hold your horses, Major," and refused to obey the order. This insubordination was most unusual. Everyone knew about it, but Commander Silverstein was a hundred miles away and, wisely, he just let it ride.

Regardless of these incidents, Major Silverstein was highly regarded by everyone who had an opportunity to work with him. Bill Shaughnessy's recollection is that Silverstein was an excellent and highly intelligent Commander who "worked like a dog. . . . He was very good at what he did," but like Colonel Turkel, he was not very concerned with being "military." These men were not professional West Pointers, yet men of skills and talents that the Army had needed.

It was not unusual that during wartime pressures, personalities and battle fatigue sometimes skewed priorities and judgment. Early in his tour of duty, Mortimer Proctor had been assigned to an officer with a fetish for sparkle, demanding that all brass buttons be constantly polished, although they actually needed polishing only if the special coating was *removed* by polishing! Even the judgment of the brilliant General Vandenberg, who recognized the importance of our work, was suspect when he ordered one of the *Westa Eins* planes shot down, forcing Lieutenant Davidson to plead, "Don't shoot down our golden goose." The *Westa Eins* — the weather flights — had been the source of our earliest daily code breaks!

And before General Vandenberg, his predecessor as Commander of 9th Air Force, Major General Clayton Bissell, also had created problems, with his behavior. Vandenberg's biography, *Hoyt S. Vandenberg, The Life of a General*, by Phillip S. Meilinger, notes:

> On one occasion he [Bissell] was displeased with the physical arrangement of the offices within his division. Bissell ordered everyone to move, and while this was taking place, all the phones were disconnected. The day was June 6, 1944.

The American military did other dumb things, too. When the American divisions in England moved into France their call signs were changed, but not the frequency they were transmitting on, so that the listening Germans knew immediately the disposition of every American unit. This made me question the "intelligence" of the military Intelligence.

But the Germans had their frustrations too. Just before the war, Jerry pulled an old Zeppelin out of mothballs to send along the Normandy coast on a "friendly" flight. There had been a rumor and they "just wanted to see" what kind of intercept equipment the British might have. Because of the number of receivers in the German operation, a large tangle of wires was produced that sent the perfectionistic officer in charge into a frenzy.

Unable to tolerate the "mess," he ordered the removal of the wires, thereby terminating all reception of British activity! While this was chaos, it was nothing compared to the nightmare von der Heydte had had to deal with when given the untrained paratroopers and pilots inexperienced in formation flying in December of '44, at the start of the Bulge.

Then, because of Hitler's paranoia, von der Heydte had fallen under suspicion for his realistic assessment of that operation. As a cousin of the officer who had attempted to assassinate the Führer with a bomb six months earlier, von der Heydte was considered a possible saboteur, reducing his credibility to zero. Any effort he made to gain necessary information for the successful execution of the drop would only increase doubt in the minds of his superiors. Perhaps he survived the war because he followed orders and jumped against all evidence to the contrary, and eventually fell into the protective hands of the Americans who respected his ability and accomplishments.

———◖◗———

We were at a critical juncture in the war, and although we sometimes felt as if we were spinning our wheels and going in many directions at once, it was, without doubt, a time of extraordinary teamwork and accomplishment — a time of pride.

———◖◗———

The Nazi sympathizers expected us and gave no resistance. . . . I got a look at the enemy face-to-face for the first time, and my mood turned somber.

Chapter Fifteen

The Other Side Has a Face

ON JANUARY 1945, my unit — Detachment A — left the luxurious accommodations of Chateau Beaumont after several months of occupation. It was a horrendous job to organize and vacate the premises because of the enormous amount of equipment, supplies, and wires. A day and a half was spent just finding the safe; we gave up on the key. In addition to the things that the Germans had left behind, we also had furniture. Like a bunch of refugees, we loaded overstuffed chairs and mattresses into our trucks and pulled out for the four-hour trip to the small village of Pargny les Reims, the center of the French champagne-producing area.

There we were billeted in Madame Maltot's spartan manor house — a long, low, cold, and cavernous structure where we dug in, literally, for there was no latrine. Unloading all our treasures, we discovered that a number of crucial items had been left behind in favor of our precious military cargo.

While other soldiers perilously hugged the freezing earth of France, we were grateful for the roof over our heads during this bitter winter month. To ward off the cold, our canteens were generously filled by the owners of the local vineyards. The people there were severely touched by the war, and the Rickets-ridden children ate hungrily from our garbage cans, their large, sunken eyes showing gratitude.

It was here that I met the laundress, an almost handsome bold-faced girl with dark hair. During the subsequent weeks of laundry pick-up and delivery of shirts, fatigues, and underwear, I became aware that she was interested in more than just washing my clothes. The local boys had warned me that she was very "difficult" and that any attempt to convince her of my charms would be a sheer waste of time, so I was surprised when she made her inclinations known.

Within a wooded grove overlooking the village was a small chapel offering a sweeping view of Rheims, shadowed by the cathedral where Jeanne D'Arc had crowned Charles VII. One night, as the harsh winter abated, the laundress and I climbed the hill and made love on the sward outside the chapel. The crystal sky was starry and the wind blew gently in the trees. Much later I came to understand why she had been receptive to me while rebuking others. With me there were no strings, no attachments, no broken hearts. I would be leaving.

At every town, our first quest had always been to find someone to do our laundry, a luxury we all insisted upon; but never again would I encounter this kind of fringe benefit.

In Pargny les Reims, as well as La Celle St. Cloud, the village of Chateau Beaumont, I made friends with a number of young boys who were later called up and sent to training camps with the French First Army. Transferred quickly to the front, many of these inexperienced young men were killed in the battle for the Colmar Pocket, near the Rhine River in northeast France, in December 1944 and January 1945.

It was at this time that some of us from 3rd RSM became more clearly aware that we were no longer working only with 9th Air Force. Mortimer Proctor recorded:

> Our whole relationship with SHAEF is a peculiar thing. On paper we are with the Ninth Air Force, but since the days in Paris we have stayed with and worked for SHAEF in particular. . . .
>
> With our link-up with SHAEF came the U/K teleprinter, which served to make us even more securely attached to them.
>
> . . . The old issue has arisen — are we to be with SHAEF or GANGWAY?

In April 1945, it was time for Detachment A to occupy enemy territory. Counter-Intelligence warned us of the difficulties we would face as we entered Germany. Silent and thoughtful about the grim uncomfortable days ahead of us, our unit piled aboard a C-47 and flew to Bad Vilbel, a spa town outside Frankfurt that had been spared bombing. We slept in the classrooms of the local school and set up our Operations Center in a huge room of the spa, where we papered the walls with large, green situation maps showing terrain features in colored relief. We were given a list of names and addresses of Nazis and ordered to go out and corral them. This roundup was considered part of our duty. We were an Intelligence unit, and, we were told, "Intelligence oversight provides you with the list, so therefore it is your responsibility to make use of it."

At first we looked at this as an adventure, a chance to see the enemy up close as the conqueror. Exuberantly we formed ourselves into little groups and piled into jeeps, chanting a stupid little ditty, *"Oh, do not let us ask, what is it? Let us go and make a visit,"* as if we were going off for a day in the country!

Our first pick-up was the German brothers Konrad and Ludwig Sussman, residing at #28 Hitlerstrasse, and Ernst and Walter Hock, from Hitlerstrasse and Heinrichstrasse, respectively. From there we went on to capture Willi and George Dittmar, at #74 Mountain Street, and Friseur Merkle — Hairdresser Merkle. Asterisks preceded the names of over 30 of them — the hard cases. Their jobs were chilling: Gestapo Service, Storm Troop Leader, Press Supervisor, Informer, Jew Baiter, Political Supervisor, Cell Leader, Union of German Girls Leader, and Harasser. They actually had designated someone to harass! The names, streets and designations evoked the image of the regime, and the echo of its cruelty.

The Nazi sympathizers expected us and gave no resistance. As we loaded them into the back of our jeeps, I got a look at the enemy face-to-face for the first time, and my mood turned somber. Wilfred Owen's words in "Strange Meeting" came back to me:

> I am the enemy you killed, my friend.
> I knew you in this dark; for so you frowned
> Yesterday through me as you jabbed and killed.
> I parried; but my hands were loath and cold.
> Let us sleep now. . . .

————◄○►————

We took our prisoners to jail, but the next morning they were released. It was quickly discovered that they were necessary for the smooth running of the town's administrative machinery. Without them nothing worked. And with them?

So relieved to be alive, many Germans were eager to surrender and would embrace or shake the hand of their captors. Some, no more than boys, just wanted to go home. They would remove their shoes as they walked on the road back to the Motherland, for a barefoot soldier meant a captured soldier, offering them some level of protection. Sometimes enemies would meet, look eyeball to eyeball, shrug, and walk away. They just couldn't kill one more human being.

Because our intercept work was winding down, we kept busy with movies, mineral baths, and booze. The local theater showed films of the recently liberated extermination camps, and the horror was beyond imagination. As more and more information became available, emotions crystallized like a fist in my gut. It was difficult not to become consumed by hatred like the Nazis had been, and for a short time, I was. My hate, which had increased during the war, became indiscriminate now as I saw what all Germans either had done or had turned their eyes from: Auschwitz, the largest killing center in the world; Bergen-Belsen, where the prisoners too weak to move shared bunks with rotting corpses; Ravensbrück, the women's camp where their bones were removed from their limbs in the name of science; Dachau, where salt water was pumped into stomachs to test survival techniques at sea; Theresienstadt, the German-made ghetto for the Jews of Europe; and Sobibor and Lublin and Treblinka and Neuengamme, and. . . . How many more camps? How many more atrocities? How many more excuses? Could this be the country of Brahms, Beethoven, and Bach? My emotions were in turmoil.

It seemed that time was standing still and the war was waiting outside. I gravitated to a bar. After the war, we were able to frequent the Peacock Club, our own little camp bar, that allowed escorted frauleins between 7:00 and 9:45 p.m. But at this time, before the end of hostilities, we had to be more adventurous and sought out local establishments. The Germans, quick to perceive that many of us were fluent in their language, struck up the inevitable conversations, and we found ourselves commingling with the enemy, a blatant violation of the "No Fraternization" rule.

Most always the local bar was alive with curiosity and attempts at gaining favors from the American victor. One particular evening a couple approached and sat down uninvited at my table, and I soon became involved in conversation with a tall, loquacious man who looked more Slavic than German. He and the tiny woman with him had straight dark hair. They were effervescent — almost breathless — with excuses and explanations. *"We never knew what was going on." "We never knew of any atrocities." "We never knew of any concentration camps." "They kept all this hidden from us." "We didn't dare ask."*

It had been a long time since the beginning of the war, when Germans were on top of the world. Initially, they had had a sense of belonging to the unconquerable Master Race. During the first three years they had amassed victories that erased the shame of their World War I surrender at Versailles and left them feeling indestructible. They enjoyed French perfume, champagne, and paté in profusion.

But as the war progressed, their cities were slowly and totally destroyed, bit by bit. The British and Americans bombed them with a one-two punch, pulverizing everything. This forced the Germans to begin building industrial structures underground. Civilian life became as difficult for them as it was for the Allies. By 1943, the bombing campaigns in Germany ebbed and flowed and eventually became increasingly more powerful, so that by late 1944 all the fighting was being done on German soil as the Russians invaded from the east. By January 1945, bombing of Germany was continuous day and night. Piles of rubble could be seen everywhere, covered by wilting flowers marking the graves of those who lay rotting beneath, unable to be retrieved for burial.

Throughout the war, police battalions of men who had been physically unable to qualify for the German army were enlisted to exterminate Jews.

They were given a choice. They chose to kill. After the first mass killings, they demanded that a better method than shooting be used because it was too messy and made them nauseated. As the Russian armies approached, the German guards marched the starving barefoot prisoners westward in the snow, shooting those who couldn't keep up. Heinrich Himmler, head of the Gestapo, ordered the marches and the murders to stop because they might interfere with his attempts to negotiate surrender terms with the Western Allies, but the command was ignored. The killing battalions preferred to keep killing.

I turned my attention to the young couple.

"Would you like to come to our place?" they asked.

I studied them with interest. This was the enemy, that much I realized. But I was young, I was curious, and I had had a few drinks. What the hell, the war's over. I didn't realize until much later why I went.

Their small apartment was dingy and confined — a kitchen, nothing more than an inlet, a living room, and a bedroom. Over cheap wine we talked about the war and how they had survived. I suspected that part of their current survival plan included their attempted friendship with me. Insisting that I stay, the man excused himself, explaining that he had an appointment.

I was alone with her. The air became heavy as I looked upon her expectant face. She stood and slowly walked to my chair. Hesitantly, she reached out her hand. We moved to the bedroom, and soon I found myself staring down at her, our bodies joined. It was over quickly, abruptly, almost angrily. There had been no need to undress; I hadn't wanted to see her. She was just there — just a receptacle for me. For a moment, as I stood over her, catching my breath, I saw Germany in all its horror.

I walked out. Outside the door I plodded into the cold night, hoping the bite of the air would cleanse me. I was disgusted with them and myself. The breath, the odor of their self-degradation, lingered. Was this degradation a precursor of Germany's future? Did they think I could protect them in some way? How could a husband sink so low as to offer up his wife?

Were we all going mad?

—◄○►—

It took a long time before I was able to understand my actions in that miserable little apartment. I never learned the German couple's motivation, but I did learn what vengeance could do. At first I saw the incident as a mere physical act, but a kind that I never wanted to participate in again. I realized that an encounter with a faceless girl was like an encounter with no one, and that I was the one being hurt. I knew there had to be more.

I wanted to look away from the truth of that night and blame it on alcohol, lust — anything other than what it was — but I knew that what it all amounted to was the rape of an entire generation of Germans through this one individual — my own hatred, my own attack, my own getting even for all they had done. Every thrust had seemed to release into the enemy all the loathing I had kept within — disgust, horror, humiliation. It was fast. It was filthy. It was finished.

"Who is the enemy?" I asked. I could hear the words of Siegfried Sassoon:

> Give me your hand, my brother, search my face;
> Look in these eyes lest I should think of shame;
> For we have made an end of all things base.
> We are returning by the road we came.

I hoped that I had, indeed, made an end of all things base.

The war had touched a raw nerve in each of us. Staff Sergeant Henry Schueftan's experience in Marburg, Germany, at war's end, with a woman dutifully wearing a swastika, elicited such rage that he had to walk away to prevent himself from striking her. She had only asked a simple question of the American serviceman, but the brutal insignia on her arm made him so furious that he was unable to speak directly to her. He told one of the other soldiers to relay the message that he would communicate only if she removed the swastika. She did, without resistance or hesitation. There was obviously no sense of conviction or commitment to the cause.

I think this probably spoke for most of the German peasants — they didn't really know what was going on. Perhaps they had simply been caught up in the magnetism and patriotism of war and the passion of victory, without the awareness of its cost or the atrocities being committed. Hitler was a powerful mentor to a generation of people that had grasped his message as water to the thirsty. We must hope that the media of today would never allow such ignorance or excuse amidst the populace.

Captain Gottlieb — first of Detachment B and then with the newly formed D — also had difficulty meeting the enemy. According to Jim Copp, Gottlieb had refused to shake hands with a German officer who was brought into the Officers Club at Fleigerlager after the war.

The repulsion lingered everywhere.

<o>

My own war experiences — danger, conflict of purpose, vulnerability, and the demand for instantaneous decision — weighed upon me. Many lives had been dependent on my actions in Detachment A. I recall a night in Germany, awaking in the middle of the night in a cold sweat.

The men of the infantry, in order to survive, had numbed themselves to the danger and horror around them, the realization that at any moment they might be shot. They understood that survival of the body required survival of the mind. Death shouted from everywhere as they struggled to keep their sanity. Many developed the "60-mile stare," a vacant look that needs no description.

As a non-combatant, however, I wasn't exposed to the daily threat of attack and possible death. I didn't have to fight to survive. I never had to become numb. Maybe that's the reason why each episode of my experiences stands out so clearly. I was afforded the luxury of reflection. I had escaped the war whole in body, if not whole in spirit. I would be going home, and not in a box.

<o>

In May of 1945, Germany was through. Its air force — the mighty Luftwaffe — was grounded; its Army was on the ropes and sliding to the canvas. It was over. They were out.

Our faceless friends on the other side sent their last message on May 7th, the day before total surrender. The text was in two parts:

It's apparent, at this moment, that we only have a few hours left to serve. We wish all radio operators, men and women, all the very, very best. Stay well and a safe journey home.
Your Old Command Signal Station.

And when they signed off, we finally knew them:

> Warrant Officer Muellere, Warrant Officer Klein, Warrant Offi-
> cer Behrendt, Staff Sergeant Batfeldt, Staff Sergeant Jipp,
> Supervisory Operator Schulte, Operator Gesinn, Operator
> Nottebrock, Operator Adrian, Operator Herbolsheimer and
> Operator Sauter. *Auf wiedersehen.*

The Luftwaffe was defunct; the 9th Air Force was bereft of compe-
tition. From the German naval base at the tip of Brittany came a final
communication: *"Calling all. This is our last cry before our eternal
silence."*

——————◦——————

Men of Detachment A in Germany, at the Remagen Bridge, 1945. From left to right (rear): Captain Hugh Davidson, John O'Hara, Arnold Franco, "Bunny" Myers, Dayle Teets, and Bill Reed; (front): Jules Wein, Felix Carpegna, Phil Roggen, and Bob Joly.

Germany, 1945 — Sergeant John Rohman of Detachment B listening to German pilots on an S-27 Hallicrafter basic Radio Telephone (R/T) receiver. Note the camouflage netting in the background.

Above: Bob Phelps and Ted Hansen in the Detachment A Intelligence Operations room in the Kurhaus-Bad Vilbel, April 1945. Note the large wall map of Europe.

Left: Actor Mickey Rooney temporarily attached for rations to Detachment B, in Germany, April 1945.

Major General Hoyt S. Vandenberg (left) presenting the Legion of Merit Award to Lieutenant Colonel Harry R. Turkel, CO of the 3rd Radio Squadron Mobile (G), May 1945, Germany.

Detachment Commanders and their adjutants of 3rd RSM meeting (in Germany?) for the only time as a group, in 1945, with their CO (in raincoat), Colonel Harry Turkel. From left to right: Heinrich (Det. C), Gottlieb (Det. D), Goodsell (Det. B), Nagel (Det. D), Brinson (Det. A), Fetter, Colonel Turkel, Hammer, Morgan, Shaugnessy (HQ), and Copp (Det. B).

```
                    LIST OF NAZIS   BAD VILBEL MAY 1945

        NAMES                  ADDRESSES                  FUNCTION

  RANFT, WILHELM          FERD. WERNERSTR. 15       CELL LEADER
  BROD, CLAERE            MARKTPLATZ 11             WOMEN'S GRP LDR
 *HENNIG, FRIEDEL         H. GOERINGSTR. 4          POLITICAL LDR
  GOEBEL, KARL  DR.       PARKSTRASSE               POLITICAL LDR
  KAISER, WILHELM         H. WESSELSTRASSE          POL. LDR, PROPAGAND
 *WOLF, ---               HOMBURGERSTRASSE          S. A. FUEHRER
  KNORR, MINNA            A. HITLE STRASSE          GESTAPO SERVICE
  SEYBOLD, WILLI          ELISABETHENSTR.           STATE ATTORNEY
  RUHL, HEINRICH          SCHULUNGSLEITER           FERD. WERNERSTR 23
  BELLER, WILLI           PETER GEMEINDERSTR.       CELL LEADER
  CAMP, HANS              ROEMERSTR. 14             CELL LEADER
 *VOELKER, HEINR.         PARKSTRASSE               ORGANIZATIONLEADER
                                                    & OLD NAZI (1923)

 *MUTH, PETER JAKOB       F. WERNERSTR. 26          GESTAPO INFORMER
  KLOESS, WILHELM         SCHUETZENSTRASSE 6        STATE ATTORNEY
  KRAMER, WILL            A. HITLERSTR. 80          S. A. FUEHRER
  SCHNEEVOGT, WILL        F. WERNERSTRASSE 27       S. A. FUHRER
  PETRI                   ORTSKRANKENKASSE          AMTSWALTER
  NEUSS, WILL             A. HITLERSTRS. 141        S. A. FUHRER
  PAULI, FRIED            HOMBURGERSTR.             GESTAPO SERVICE
  WAMSER, WALTER          A. HITLERSTRS. 181        S. A. FUHRER
 *ORMANCIN, FRIEDEL       A HITLERSTR. 185          S.A. FUHRER WITH
                                                    SPECIAL POWERS

  FRITZEL, WILLI          A HITLERSTRS. 136         CELL LEADER
  FISCHER, AUGUST         A HITLERSTRS. 82          GAULEITERS AIDE
  SCHWARTZ, KARL          A HITLERSTRS. 110         VERTRAUENSMANN
                                                    DER GEWERBETREIB

  BECKER, HEINR.          F. WERNERSTR. 42          S. A. FUHRER
 *LANG, WILHEM            ERZWEG 18                 POLITICAL LDR.
  MUTH, KARL              P. GEMEIDERSTR.           POLITCAL LDR.
 *DICKHARDT, ANNA         SCHULSTRS                 WOMEN'S ORG.
  FENN                    ROEMERSTR. 6              GESTAPO, AND SS
  WALTZ, WILHELM          A HITLERSTRS.             BUILDING COMMISSION
 *GOBEL, JEAN             ALBANUSSTR.               S.A. FUHRER
                                                    JEW PERSECUTOR

  SCHMIDT, OTTO           A HITLERSTR               BEIGE RDNETER
 *DOERR, OTT              A HITLERSTR.              STADTBAUMEISTER
                                                    INTIMUS DER FUE-
                                                    HRUNG

  KRONER, PHILIPP         A HITLERSTR.              AMTSWALTER
 *GILBERT, DORIS          LOHSTRASSE                BDM FUEHRERIN
 *VELTEN, LOTTE           ERZWEG 24                 BDM FUEHRERIN
  OHLEMUTZ, JAKOB         H. WESSELSTR.   4         POLITCAL LDR
 *GEIST, WILHELM          TAUNUSTR 1                POLITICAL LDR
  WOLFF, PAUL             A HITLERSTRS. 110         POLITCAL LDR.
```

Bad Vilbel, Germany, May 1945 — The address list (continued on next two pages) of local Nazi leaders and their functions. 3rd RSM imprisoned some, but all were quickly released under orders from Supreme Headquarters (SHAEF) in Frankfurt.

CONTINUED

NAMES	ADDRESSES	FUNCTION
WEIL, FRISEUSE	H. GOERINGSTR.	GESTAPO SERVICE
*JAMIN, BERNHARD	A HITLERSTRS. 9	OFFICIAL GERMAN WORKERS FRONT
*RACH, HEINR.	A. HITLERSTR. SCHULE	S.A. FUHRER
WUEST, ERNST	BERGSTR.	OFFICIAL GERMAN WORKERS FRONT
*SUSSMANN, KONRAD	A HITLERSTRS. 28	S. A. FUHRER BESTAPO SERVICE
*SUSSMANN, LUDWIG	A HITLERSTRS. 28	POLITCAL LDR
MARKWORT, AUGUST	BAHNHOFSTR.	CELL LEADER
VOELKER, WILHEM	RINDENBURGSTR.	AMTSLEITER
GRIMM, JEAN	PARKSTR.	POLITCAL LDR
GRUENHAUPT, WILHELM	ELISABETHENSTR. 36	AMTSLEITER
MERKEL, HEINR.	ELISABETHENSTRS. 36	AMTSLEITER
HAPPEL, JAKOB	BERGSTR.	S. A. FUEHRER
*DITTMAR, WILLI	BERGSTR. 74	S. A FUEHRER
*DITTMAR, GEORG	A HITLERSTRASSE 10	POL. LEITER
KAESER	F. WERNERSTRS. 9	POL. LEITER
FUHR, FRAU	F. WERNERSTRS. 20	WOMEN'S ORG LDR
SIECK, ANNA	A HITLERSTRS	WOMEN'S ORG LDR
*GUYOT, ERNST DR	A. HITLERSTR 160	S. A. FUHRER
APPEL, MARTIN	A HITLERSTR.	S. A. FUHRER
*SCHUTT	H. WESSELSTR	NSKK FUHRER
*HOCK, ERNST	A HITLERSTR. 21	POL. LEITER
*HOCK, WALTER	HEINRICHSTR.	POL. LEITER
HARTMANN, FERD	A HITLERSTR. 107	CELL LEADER
KRONER, ANDREAS	D. ECKARTSTR.	S. A. FUHRER
*FRIED, JOSEF	BERGSTR.	POL. LEITER, S.A. SPECIAL DUTY
MARTINI, HEINRICH	A HITLERSTR.	PRESSELEITER
OBERNHUBER, ELSE	LOHSTR.	POL. LEITERIN
SCHAUB, FRITZ	HANAUERSTR.	ORTSGRUPPEN - LEITER
LAMP, GEB. DITTMAR	A HITLERSTR.	INFORMER
JAEGER, HEINRICH	A HITLERSTR.	INFORMER
PFEIFFER, PHILIPP	H. GOERINGSTR.	BUSINESS MANAGER OF NSDAP
SAUERWEIN, WILHELMINE	A HITLERSTR.	INFORMER
SCHAEFER, GEB. SAUERWEIN	A HITLERSTR.	ACTIVE POLITICALLY
BRANDEL, HENNI	BERGSTR.	INFORMER
MUELLER, JULIUS	A HITLERSTRS. 132	SS MEMBER
GILBERT	A HITLERSTRS	PARTY COURIER
*MERKLE, FRISEUR	A HITLERSTR.	NSKK FUHRER-COURIER
ZUTT, FRAU	H. WESSELSTR	WOMEN'S ORG. LD R
DERWORT, ELISE	WILHELMSTR	WOMEN'S ORG. LDR
OCHS, GEB. KLOESS	HINDENBURGSTR.	CELL LEADER

The address list (continued) of local Nazi leaders and their functions.

NAMES	ADDRESS	FUNCTION
WEINERT, ALEXANDER	SCHOENE AUSSICHT	AMTSLEITER
BROD, GEORG	A HITLERSTR	POL. LEITER
*JOST, HEINR. II	A. HITLERSTR.	S.A. FUHRER, INFORMER JEW BAITER
REUKAUF, ALBERT	F. WERNERSTR. 17	KASSENWART, AMTS-LEITER
OBERSCHWESTER DES KRANKENHAUSES		POL - HETZERIN ANGEBERIN
REITZ, KARL	A HITLERSTR.	STATE ATTORNEY
SCHMIDT, FRAU DR	A HITLERSTR	WOMEN'S ORG.
HOEFFNER, FRITZ	KURHAUS	INFORMER
*MUELLER, CHRISTIAN	A. HITLERSTR.	JEW BAITER
KAUTZ, LEHRER	A HITLERSTR.	SCHULUNGS LEITER
HINKEL, REINHARD	BERGSTRASSE	S. A. FUHRER
DIEHL, GEB. SCHMIDT	LANDGRABENSTR.	WOMEN'S ORG.
KUNZ, FRAU	RITTERSTR.	" "
PFEIFFER, KARL	H. GORINGSTR	POL. LEITER
*HEUSSEL, WENER	BERGSTRASE	RECHSTBERATER, HETZER
EISENHARDT, MARTIN	A HITLERSTR	ORTSGRUPPENLEITER
BELLER GEB. SCHOEN	P GEMEINDERSTR	WOMENTS ORG
*WENIG, GEB. JAMIN	A HITLERSTR.	WOMEN 'S ORG
*WALZ, THEODOR	A HITLERSTR.	AMTSLEITER INFORMER

The address list (continued) of local Nazi leaders and their functions.

```
                    RASTER INTEICEPT 7/5/45

FREQUENCY:  3082 KCS    T.O.O:  0759         T.O.I:  0819

INDICATORS:  HCKP MO    CALLSIGN: UEG

TEXT:  (PART ONE OF TWO PARTS)  UNSERE TAETIGKEIT WIRD JETZT WAHRSCHEINL+
LICH NOCH STUNDEN BEMESSEN SEIN X VIR WUENSCHEN ALLEN FUNKER UND FUNK-
ERINNEN ALLES ALLES GUTE STOP BEEIST GESUND UND KOMMT GUT IN DIE
HEIMAT   EURE ALE HAUPTFUNKSTELLE

                    RASTER INTERCEPTS
DATE:  7/5/45     CALLSIGN: ---                T.O.I: 0822
T.O.O: ---        INDICATOR:  UATS VH          FREQ: 3082 KCS
TEXT:  (PART TWO OF TWO PART MESSAGE)  UFFZ MUELLERE UFFZ KLEIN UFFZ
       BEHRENDT STABGFR BATFELDT STABGFR JIPP HAUPTHELF SCHULTE
       OBHELF GESINN OBHELF NOTTEBROCK OBHELF ADRIAN OBHELF HERBOLS-
       HEIMER OBHELF SAUTER   AUFWIEDERSEHEN
```

The last German message intercepted and decoded by Detachment A, 3rd RSM, on May 7, 1945. The war ended with the German surrender on May 8th.

Lowering the antenna at Weimar, *ca.* May 8, 1945.

The huge portal of the University of Nancy dwarfs Arnold Franco, the entering student, July 1945.

A copy of the Belgian Fourragere Award to Detachments B and D, permitting them to wear it over their right shoulder "when in proper uniform."

11 August 1945
Date issued

Headquarters XXIX Tactical Air Command

MUNICH ⑨ GERMANY

CITATION FOR

The Belgian Fourragere 1940

Albert J. Gruber   Staff Sergeant   32690424

UNITED STATES ARMY, for meritorious service in Belgium from 1 October 1944 to 15 January 1945 inclusive.

1. His Royal Highness and Prince-Regent of Belgium has twice cited the XXIX Tactical Air Command in Orders of the Day of the Belgian Army-Decision No. 717, dated 7 July 1945, for meritorious service in Belgium from 1 October 1944 to 15 January 1945 inclusive, in connection with military operations against the enemy.

2. The unceasing and heroic efforts of the Officers and Enlisted personnel of the units of the XXIX Tactical Air Command permitted this headquarters to organize and prescribe the missions so effectively carried out against the enemy. Yours was a decisive and glorious part in the defeat of the enemy during the Battle of the Ardennes and you have helped immeasurably in the liberation of Belgium.

3. For these two citations, His Royal Highness the Prince-Regent of Belgium has awarded you The Belgium Fourragere (1940). This certificate authorizes you the right to wear this Fourragere as a visible token of your military virtue and the gratitude of the peoples of Belgium. The War Department has approved the awarding of The Belgian Fourragere (1940) with citation per War Department Cable (AG-WAR-WX 32845 dated 15 July 1945).

4. It is to be noted that having been an original member of your organization during the period 1 October 1944 to 15 January 1945 inclusive, you are authorized by the War Department to wear the Fourragere over the right shoulder when in proper uniform in any branch or echelon of the United States Army, Navy, or Marine Corps establishments.

R. E. NUGENT
Brigadier General, U. S. Army
Commanding

FERDINAND GOTTLIEB, Captain, Signal Corps
Unit Commander

Detachment "D" 3rd Radio Squadron Mobile (G)
Air Organization

(This citation not valid unless signed and sealed by Unit Commander.)

HONORABLE DISCHARGE

1. LAST NAME - FIRST NAME - MIDDLE INITIAL	2. ARMY SERIAL NO.	3. GRADE	4. ARM OR SERVICE	5. COMPONENT
FRANCO ARNOLD C	12 142 235	CPL	AAF	ERC

6. ORGANIZATION	7. DATE OF SEPARATION	8. PLACE OF SEPARATION
DET A 3 RD SQ	28 DEC 45	SEP CTR FT DIX NJ

9. PERMANENT ADDRESS FOR MAILING PURPOSES	10. DATE OF BIRTH	11. PLACE OF BIRTH
107-19 119 ST RICHMOND HILL NY	27 SEP 23	NY NY

12. ADDRESS FROM WHICH EMPLOYMENT WILL BE SOUGHT	13. COLOR EYES	14. COLOR HAIR	15. HEIGHT	16. WEIGHT	17. NO. DEPEND.
SEE 9	BR	BLK	5/9	170 LBS.	0

18. RACE	19. MARITAL STATUS	20. U.S. CITIZEN	21. CIVILIAN OCCUPATION AND NO.
WHITE W NEGRO OTHER (specify)	SINGLE X MARRIED OTHER (specify)	YES X NO	STUDENT X2 02

MILITARY HISTORY

22. DATE OF INDUCTION	23. DATE OF ENLISTMENT	24. DATE OF ENTRY INTO ACTIVE SERVICE	25. PLACE OF ENTRY INTO SERVICE
	11 SEP 42	4 MAR 43	NYC

SELECTIVE SERVICE DATA ▶	26. REGISTERED YES NO X	27. LOCAL S.S. BOARD NO. NONE	28. COUNTY AND STATE NONE	29. HOME ADDRESS AT TIME OF ENTRY INTO SERVICE SEE 9

30. MILITARY OCCUPATIONAL SPECIALTY AND NO.	31. MILITARY QUALIFICATION AND DATE (i.e., infantry, aviation and marksmanship badges, etc.)
CRYPTANALYP 808	RIFLE M1 EXP CARB MKM 147 14 MAY 44

32. CENTRAL EUROPE NORMANDY NORTHERN FRANCE RHINELAND
GO 33 WD 45 AS AMENDED

33. DECORATIONS AND CITATIONS
AMERICAN SERVICE MEDAL   EAME SV MEDAL   GOOD CONDUCT MEDAL
WORLD WAR 2 VICTRY MEDAL

34. WOUNDS RECEIVED IN ACTION
NONE

35. LATEST IMMUNIZATION DATES				36. SERVICE OUTSIDE CONTINENTAL U.S. AND RETURN		
SMALLPOX	TYPHOID	TETANUS	OTHER (specify)	DATE OF DEPARTURE	DESTINATION	DATE OF ARRIVAL
9OCT45	8MAR45	28MAR45	NONE	24 MAY 44	ETO	25 MAY 44
			38. HIGHEST GRADE HELD	2 DEC 45	US	21 DEC 45

37. TOTAL LENGTH OF SERVICE						
CONTINENTAL SERVICE			FOREIGN SERVICE			
YEARS	MONTHS	DAYS	YEARS	MONTHS	DAYS	
1	2	27	1	6	28	CPL

39. PRIOR SERVICE
NONE

40. REASON AND AUTHORITY FOR SEPARATION
CONVENIENCE OF THE GOVERNMENT AR 615-365 15 DEC 44 & RR 1-1 DEMOBILIZATION

41. SERVICE SCHOOLS ATTENDED	42. EDUCATION (Years)		
CRYPTANALYPT WARRENTON VA 1944 ASTP MICH STATE COL 1943	Grammar 8	High School 4	College 4

PAY DATA

43. LONGEVITY FOR PAY PURPOSES			44. MUSTERING OUT PAY		45. SOLDIER DEPOSITS	46. TRAVEL PAY	47. TOTAL AMOUNT, NAME OF DISBURSING OFFICER
YEARS 3	MONTHS 3	DAYS 18	TOTAL $300	THIS PAYMENT $100	NONE	$ 3.95	187.37 J HARRIS COL FD

INSURANCE NOTICE

IMPORTANT — IF PREMIUM IS NOT PAID WHEN DUE OR WITHIN THIRTY-ONE DAYS THEREAFTER, INSURANCE WILL LAPSE. MAKE CHECKS OR MONEY ORDERS PAYABLE TO THE TREASURER OF THE U. S. AND FORWARD TO COLLECTIONS SUBDIVISION, VETERANS ADMINISTRATION, WASHINGTON 25, D. C.

48. KIND OF INSURANCE	49. HOW PAID			50. Effective Date of Allotment Discontinuance	51. Date of Next Premium Due (One month after 50)	52. PREMIUM DUE EACH MONTH	53. INTENTION OF VETERAN TO
Nat. Serv. X U.S. Govt. None	Allotment X	Direct to V.A.		31 DEC 45	31 JAN 46	$ 6.50	Continue Continue Only Discontinue X

54.	55. REMARKS (This space for completion of above items or entry of other items specified in W. D. Directives)
RIGHT THUMB PRINT	LAPEL BUTTON ISSUED ASR CSCORE 2 SEP 45 68

56. SIGNATURE OF PERSON BEING SEPARATED	57. PERSONNEL OFFICER (Type name, grade and organization - signature)
	WHITE CAPT AC

WD AGO FORM 53 55
1 November 1944

This form supersedes all previous editions of
WD AGO Forms 53 and 55 for all persons

Arnold Franco's discharge paper. Franco had received the American Service Medal, World War II Victory Medal, EAME SV Medal, and the Good Conduct Medal.

The Christmas card sent by Major Mortimer Proctor from Bad Vilbel, Germany, to Arnold Franco, regretting the lack of adequate promotions of the Intelligence Staff, January 1946.

SEASONS GREETINGS

You must be home by now — I hope so, in any case. If I didn't know that you are better off where you are, I should wish you back here. As it is, you got out just in time. We have already had more than enough of snow and freezing temperatures. But we do miss you.

The place is scarcely recognizable now — not only have vast numbers of the men left, but also Major Brown, Captain Cox and Captain Davidson as well. As a result of all this drainage I have been obliged to take over

Merry Christmas

AND

A HAPPY NEW YEAR

MORTIMER PROCTOR

DETACHMENT "A"
2d Radio Squadron Mobile (G)
Bad Vilbel (Germany)

The skeleton that is left. But I don't relish the job much, and will head for home on the first ship that will have me.

I hope you know how we all hated to see you go. If I can say so without sounding pompous, you did more than an outstanding job. It was always painful to me and to Capt. Danielson that you and so many others with you joined the Organization so late that you couldn't be promoted at the rate you deserved. Write if you have a moment — Mort

U. S. EMBASSY OFFICIAL DECORATED

IN a ceremony held at the residence of the French Military and Naval Attaché, Harry R. Turkel, First Secretary of the U. S. Embassy and expert in its Economic Unit, received the high military decoration of the Croix de Guerre, with gold star, that he was awarded by General De Gaulle for heroism in the invasions of North Africa and Normandy. Mr. Turkel, then a Lieutenant Colonel in the U. S. Army, was wounded in the campaign in France. He received the decoration at the hands of Captain de Fragata Rouvellou of the French Embassy, and the ceremony was attended by French Ambassador Lescuyer, Mrs. Turkel and the two young Turkel children, and members of the French and U. S. Embassy staffs.

After release from the Army, Mr. Turkel returned to his duties in the Department of State in Washington, and was assigned to the U. S. Embassy in Mexico in September 1947.

NOSOTROS   105
México, mayo 8 de 1948

Colonel Harry R. Turkel and his family, after Turkel received the *Croix de Guerre* at the French Embassy, May 1948.

*It was time to move from the past and the fight for survival
to the reality of a future and the ability to make plans.*

LONDON

AMSTERDAM
Antwerp
BERLIN
BRUSSELS

PARIS

F

Munich

VIE

BERN

Chapter Sixteen

Remains of the Day

Marseille

CORSICA

ROME

Anzio

Nap

SARDINIA

*HAVE JOURNEYED with him and only now do I begin to
understand why he wanted to be here. We have been cold,
wet, exhausted, and terrified, and yet we have shared a bond
of pride as I observed how he grew into a man.*

Algiers

Bône
Bizerte

————— ◄◉► —————

Our Commander offered furloughs — Paris immediately, or
England at a later date. I chose Paris. The festivities awaited.
Boarding the train, I discovered it to be a "Have" and "Have Not"
mélange. Allied servicemen filled the two rear comfortable European
coaches. The rest of the world packed into the "40 and 8s," quasi pas-

senger/cattle cars of the First World War designed to haul 40 men and 8 horses. These were jammed with the recently freed concentration camp inmates, forced laborers, and prisoners of war.

Taking a circuitous route through southeast Belgium because direct rail service to Paris had not yet been reestablished, the sea of people outside the cars no longer appeared remote and faceless. As we halted at each town, the tattered — still wearing striped camp uniforms, shredded filthy clothing, or faded military garb — stumbled off into the waiting mass of anxious faces to sobbing reunions, shattering grief, and hopeless shrugs, giving slow, negative shakes of the head when asked about someone who hadn't returned. The contrasting scenes of happiness and utter grief were too painful for me. By the time we arrived at Liege, I could no longer stand the emotional ups and downs and pulled the shade.

Paris was still the city I had remembered. Madame "Madam" welcomed me with open arms, as did the Lorthiois family and lovely Christiane. The war had passed over all of them like a strange cloud, and the future lay ahead, though on an indefinable landscape.

Time was the difficulty now. My unit, and the U.S. Army in general, was confronted with an occupational vacuum. To fill this void, the command thought up activities to keep our idle hands from making mischief. One of their ideas came to me custom-made — a six week course in the study of French literature offered at the University of Nancy. I jumped at the chance, and spent that summer sitting in the sunny arcades discussing Molière, Flaubert, Hugo, and Zola.

The wonderful hours passed quickly, and I found myself back at Bad Vilbel, northeast of Frankfurt-am-Main, monitoring the Russians. It was August 1945. The bombs had been dropped on Hiroshima and Nagasaki, and the war was over. I was alternating between the past and the future — the known and the unknown — and the words of Britain's World War I poet Herbert Read echoed in my mind:

> The universe swaying between Nothing and Being and life faltering like a clock's tick between a pendulum's coming and going.

After so long a struggle it was difficult to adjust to the daily life of peace. Henry Schueftan recalls his reaction the day after the war ended, when he saw a truck parked perpendicular to a building. This was strictly *verboten* because it was a camouflage violation, so he immediately began looking for the driver to get it moved, when he realized it was no longer necessary.

While we were awaiting orders, the government drew up a point system to determine who was to be discharged first. The clerical staff began assessing points relative to the amount of time served. Because of my longevity in the European theater, I had accumulated 85 points, the exact number needed, so I found myself near the top of the list to be sent home. I was dispatched from Bad Vilbel to Bad Kissingen, a spa town noted for its stimulating baths and masseurs, where I joined a group of short-termers to be sorted out and entrained. There Detachments B, C, and D were consolidated into one detachment, known as B, to await their release. It was a very pleasant time of wining and dining.

For some unexplainable reason, the new unit had acquired "mascots" — two beautiful 18-year-old Russian girls. Feeling older and wiser, we all assumed the role of their protector, but this was a difficult task because they didn't always want protection. I'm not sure anyone in our unit wanted them protected either.

Meanwhile, our Captain Hugh Davidson was attached to an outfit whose sole purpose was to get the men home. These soldiers were from many units who had nothing in common except their dislike for the Colonel in charge who strutted around in confiscated enemy furs. Davidson, as transportation officer responsible for getting everybody on a ship home, remembers:

> The instructions said that all articles of fur had to be fumigated before you got on the boat. We had several fur pieces including the Colonel's hat and big coat that he was very proud of. We went over to the fumigating place that was run by German POWs. They steamed those furs for about thirty minutes and they all shrank to nothing. The Colonel saw his hat shrunken so small that he couldn't even get his fist in it. His long overcoat was very tight and only came down to the waist. "I've been fucked," he screamed. Later I went for a hair cut and tried to pay the customary fifty cents but the barber said, "No sir,

Captain Davidson, you'll never pay me for any hair cut I give
you, not after what you did to the Colonel's coat and hat!"

———————◄o►———————

My orders arrived. It was time to go home. It was time to move from
the past and the fight for survival to the reality of a future and the ability
to make plans. I was so grateful to be alive, but at the same time I knew
that I was probably leaving the most exciting time my life. It was a bitter-
sweet moment.

> I stand on this hill and accept
> The pleasure my flesh dictates
> I count not kisses nor take
> Too serious a view of tobacco.
>
> I stand on this hill and accept
> The flowers at my feet and the deep
> Beauty of the still tarn;
> Chance that gave me a crutch and a view
> Gave me these.

Poet Herbert Read was able to say in the First World War what I now
felt, overlooking the countryside, reflecting on the glow of my cigar and
the ash of my past. I was weary. This had been more than the passing of a
few years; it had been a discovery and confrontation with a Self.

I boarded the train, but this time the accommodations weren't luxurious
coaches. We were jammed into the 40 and 8s, 20 to a car. As the French
countryside swam past, the words of the popular song "Sentimental Journey" rang in my ears and the meaning hit home. I was mesmerized by the
stillness of the landscape, in which nothing seemed to have changed — yet
I knew it had. Like the cow hanging in the tree in Avranches that belied
the truth of its death, the serene countryside lay before me also masking
reality. After two days on the rails with comfort stops and K-rations, I
eagerly greeted Marseilles where I promenaded the Cannebiere — the
main boulevard — in the sunlight.

From there I boarded a Liberty ship, a mass-produced vessel dreamed
up by Henry Kaiser at the start of the war to meet a crushing need.

Slipping our moorings, we headed west through the Straits of Gibraltar, settling down for an uneventful trip. Word came that storms were raging in the mid-Atlantic, so the Captain veered south, hoping to skirt their main force; but the edge of the front struck the ship day after day, flinging everything about. The waves whipped and the heavens howled, and during the night the mess hall's dinnerware smashed to the deck in a violent roll. The hold was fetid with vomit, and men lunged through darkened gangways seeking air. I curled up in an anti-aircraft gun mount rather than sleep below. It was cold, but at least I could breathe.

Two miserable weeks at sea brought us to the New York skyline and Bartholdi's Lady of Liberty. As we steered for Newark, where the land and city were bleak with the dark gray cold of December, I stood on deck recalling Kipling's poem "The Return":

> Peace is declared, an' I return
>> To 'Ackneystadt, but not the same;
> Things 'ave transpired which made me learn
>> The size and meanin' of the game.
> I did no more than others did,
>> I don't know where the change began.
> I started as an average kid,
>> I finished as a thinkin' man.

As uninviting as the weather made America appear, it was home — my home — and now I was questioning if I had really lived all those experiences of the past three years. Europe seemed to be another planet.

With gear on my back, I stumbled down the gangway and entrained to Fort Dix for mustering out, eager to get on with life. The clerical staff on base wasn't interested in efficiency or our desires, and a riot of shouting broke out. The milling combat veterans who had fought their way across Europe had had their fill. Confronting the headquarters staff with curses and open mutiny, they got attention and processing speeded up. Then it was finally my turn.

With discharge papers in hand, I ran to the nearest telephone and called my folks. To my father I announced that I was calling from Paris. After a moment's pause, the other end of the line erupted with, "The hell you say. You're right here. I can hear you too clearly. Come on home."

——◄o►——

As we boarded the train to the city, I could feel his eagerness. Taking the subway transfers to the E train, we once again passed the signs for Richmond Hill and Kew Gardens. We had come full circle as he read the familiar names that had warmed him in the London underground, but this time he was home.

At last we caught the bus that took us to his old stop, and ran the rest of the way, lugging his barracks bag on our back. The front door opened, and golden light poured across the stoop. The welcoming arms of his family enveloped us. It was Christmas Eve.

———◆◇◆———

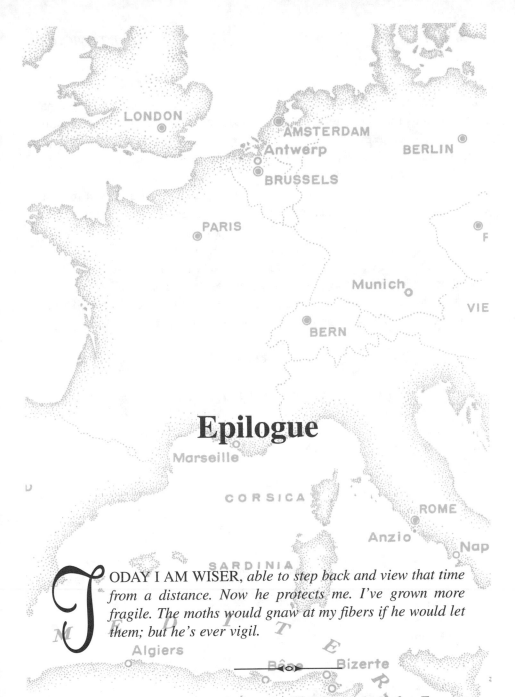

Epilogue

*T*ODAY I AM WISER, *able to step back and view that time from a distance. Now he protects me. I've grown more fragile. The moths would gnaw at my fibers if he would let them; but he's ever vigil.*

———◄●►———

In June 1994, I boarded the *Queen Elizabeth II* for France. Smooth, majestic, powerful, the *Queen* took the veterans of World War II back for the 50th anniversary of D-Day.

We were put up at a Paris hotel not far from the *Champs Elysées*, where we would later march two blocks to the sacred flame underneath the *Arc de Triomphe*. That morning, the hotel management had informed us that the veterans were to be regaled with France's best champagne before the event. And so, thoroughly "in our cups," we boarded a bus for the parade's start, where we formed up in uniform. We marched to the *Arc de Triomphe*, halted, and stood at attention in ranks as an old French General limped past, stopping to shake each hand. When my turn came, his look pierced me, eyeing the medals on my chest. I murmured, "*Mon General.*"

The French were wonderful. They do remember, and they are grateful.

When we had visited Omaha Beach, we sat proudly during the ceremony. Later, we visited the *Café de la Paix* on the *Champs Elysées*, where I sat at the same table as I had during the war, and in the same uniform. I ordered a bottle of vintage French wine to toast my return to Paris.

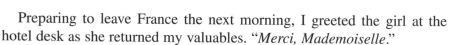

Preparing to leave France the next morning, I greeted the girl at the hotel desk as she returned my valuables. "*Merci, Mademoiselle.*"

In reply, she took me by the hand, and tears filled my eyes as she responded, "No, sir, it is for us to thank you."

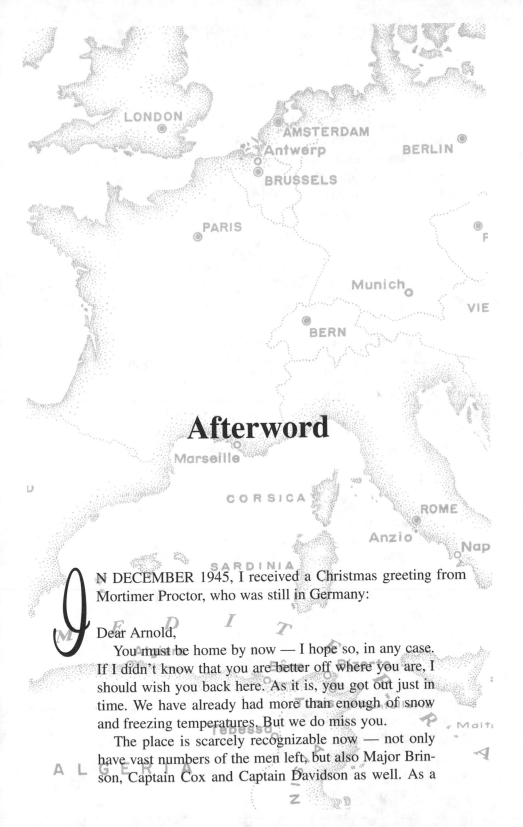

Afterword

*J*N DECEMBER 1945, I received a Christmas greeting from Mortimer Proctor, who was still in Germany:

Dear Arnold,

You must be home by now — I hope so, in any case. If I didn't know that you are better off where you are, I should wish you back here. As it is, you got out just in time. We have already had more than enough of snow and freezing temperatures. But we do miss you.

The place is scarcely recognizable now — not only have vast numbers of the men left, but also Major Brinson, Captain Cox and Captain Davidson as well. As a result of all this, I have been obliged to take over the skeleton that is left, but I don't relish the job much and will head for home on the first ship that will have me.

I hope you know how we all hated to see you go. If I can say so without sounding pompous, you did more than an outstanding job. It was always painful to me and to Captain Davidson that you and so many others with you joined the organization so late that you couldn't be promoted at the rate you deserved.

Write if you have a moment. —
Mortimer Proctor.

After the war, much valuable information was obtained by prisoner interrogation. A German pilot finally explained the mystery of the transmission "*Periscope up*," that had gnawed at our unit. In the wartime circumstances, he was unable to communicate with his pregnant wife, and when she gave birth, the sex of his child was transmitted through this message.

Sometimes we simply tried too hard to break a code!

It was in 1997 that I again returned to Europe, to seek out some of the places that had been occupied by the other detachments. In Belgium, I followed a double-rutted gravel-filled road to the bottom of a valley. Looming before me stood a majestic gate tower and Chateau La Commanderie. It was as beautiful as the guys from D had said. On the left of the drawbridge, which didn't draw, the moat was filled with clear running water; but on the right, it was stagnant with floating green algae. Cautiously, the owner answered the door, and upon hearing my request drew a map in the gravel of the driveway to the residence of Countess Fiorella Ferretti di Castel Ferrato, with an encouraging remark to seek her out: *Tant qu' ancien combattant americain vous avez tous les droits* — "As an old American veteran, all doors are open."

Despite his directions, I immediately got lost, but fate bailed me out. Before me stood an imposing residence. Not wanting to waste more time, I decided to ring the bell and ask for help. When *madame* heard my story, she said, "Oh, Fiorella, she's a good friend of mine. I'll phone her." At the very moment she re-entered the house, a car drove up and a couple got out, looked at me inquiringly, and walked inside. While waiting on the porch, I mused at my good fortune at having stumbled upon Fiorella's friend and wondered whether life would continue to present more coincidences — and what the chances were of the woman who had just arrived turning out to be Madame Fiorella herself.

Within a minute the three came out, and the woman asked, "Are you looking for me? I am Fiorella Ernst." I tried to contain my excitement as I explained about Detachment D and Captain Fred Gottlieb, its Commander, whose unit had occupied her grandmother's castle near the end of the war. With tear-filled eyes, she invited me to her home where eager conversations and recollections ensued. Fiorella was flooded with memories as she viewed the 1944 photos that had been taken by Captain Gottlieb, and she in turn shared her photos and documents of that era. While the Germans had occupied her grandmother's castle prior to the Americans, Fiorella and Antoine, her future husband, had taken photos of the enemy from the attic window. She recalled that it had been a very dangerous time for her and her grandmother who kept to their rooms because the Germans were so drunk on French wine that the officers couldn't maintain discipline; they finally abandoned the troops without anyone in command. The day Captain Gottlieb had arrived to acquisition the castle for the Americans was a day of relief and remembrance:

> He was a charming and disciplined soldier, not like the Germans. He was very considerate of me and my grandmother, and when the Germans broke through in the Ardennes he sent a messenger warning us to be careful. After several anxious days the Nazis were pushed back. We thanked all of these brave American soldiers and prayed for them.

—◄○►—

That same year — 1997 — Mary Silverstein, wife of Major Ted Silverstein, Commanding Officer of Detachment B, told me that my manuscript put to rest a question that had haunted her for over 50 years. While reading *Code to Victory* to her 92-year-old husband, she discovered why she had never received any letters from him, her boyfriend, during the preinvasion period. It was the time when General Eisenhower had held up the mail — the same time my mother had been so frantic about my silence. "I am so grateful," she said. "It is a question that has hurt me all this time. I thought that he was injured or had found someone else. By the time the war was over, Ted couldn't remember."

From a 1998 vantage point, looking back to that time of world conflict, I can each day more fully appreciate how fortunate I was to have not only survived the war, but survived intact. Many years ago, I was being examined by an ophthalmologist who asked if I had ever had an injury to my left eye. As I started to say "No," I remembered the incident when I had peered out of my foxhole and was struck by a piece of flak. Sharing the story with him, he explained that I had no vision between 10 and 12 o'clock and that my eye had gotten used to "seeing" around the damaged area — a small price to pay, it would seem, by comparison.

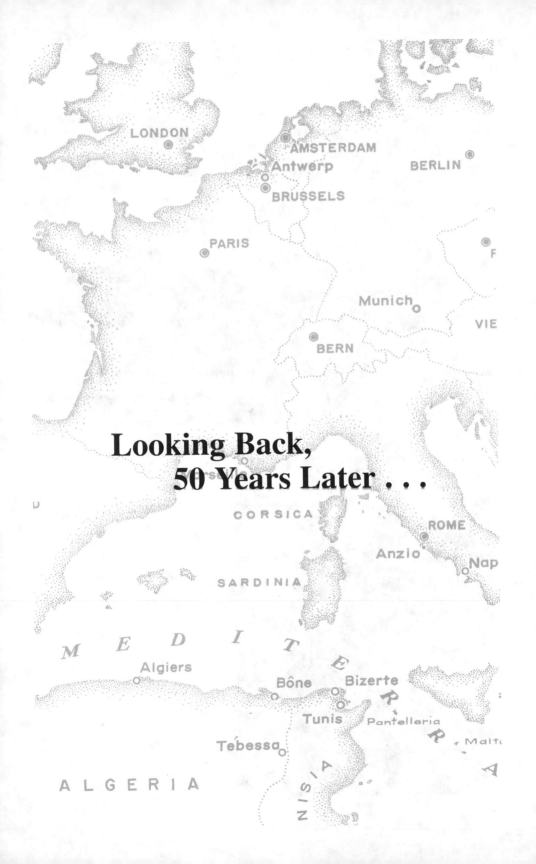

Looking Back,
50 Years Later . . .

Above: In May 1994, Arnold Franco was aboard the *Queen Elizabeth II*, on the way to the 50th anniversary celebration in France. In the forefront is Walter Cronkite.

Left: Arnold Franco at the 9th Air Force Boardroom on the *Queen Elizabeth II*, 1994.

Above: Arnold Franco and Andy Rooney at the 9th Air Force Boardroom, on the *Queen Elizabeth II*, 1994.

Left: Henry Schueftan, 1995.

Below: Arnold Franco (l) and Fred Gottlieb (r), 1996, after Franco pinned a Normandy Landing Medal on Gottlieb's left collar.

Above: Peter White (left) and Arnold Franco at White's home in Box Hill, Long Island, designed by his grandfather, Stanford White, the noted architect, 1996.

Left: Bill Shaugnessy (left), Ted Silverstein (center), age 93, and Arnold Franco, in July 1996 in Chicago.

Arnold Franco (left) and William Turkel, son of Harry Turkel, CO of 3rd RSM, 1996.

Arnold Franco and Diane Putney of the Office of Air Force History, Bolling AFB, Washington, D.C., 1996.

La Chataigneraie in 1996, now an administrative and social center for the local community.

In 1996 the "Intelligence" tower of La Chataigneraie stands the test of time.

Below: Arnold Franco's letter to various squadron mates after discovering confirmation that Detachment A's code break on the German paratroop drop was the clearest indication Supreme Headquarters had of the German offensive.

From: Arnold C. Franco   Christmas Day 1996
      63 Wall St. N>Y>C> 10005
      (212) 269-1180 Fax 269-1944
To: Interested Parties

        In mid 1996 the National Security Administration (N.S.A.)
        declassified and released to the National Archives in
        College Park, Md. a veritable host of previously TOP
        SECRET documents. Included therein is "ULTRA":Indications
        of German Offensive W.W. II battle of the Ardennes."
        I have excerpted parts of this document to send you.

        I think you will find it to be most interesting reading.
        Please excuse the various penned notations I added.

Above: The American Cemetery at Omaha Beach, April 1997. Arnold Franco is at the grave of Richard Solderholm, killed June 9, 1944. Solderholm was the first casualty of 3rd Radio Squadron Mobile.

Right: Sergeant Albert Gruber, 1997.

April 1997, Normandy — Mayor Louis Le Vin (middle) of Cricqueville-en-Bessin, next to the monument erected to the 354th Fighter Group. Note that the 3rd Radio Squadron foxholes were about 1/4-mile to the left.

The War Museum at La Gleize, Belgium. Arnold Franco and his Belgian "students," in September 1997, after a lecture on the Battle of the Bulge.

In September 1997, Monsieur and Madame Martens joined Arnold Franco on the terrace of their Chateau at Jehanster, Belgium (occupied by Detachment B after fleeing Jalhay in December 1944).

Arnold Franco, September 1997, in front of the Gatehouse at Chateau La Commanderie, Fouron St. Pierre (Sint Pieters Voeren), Belgium, Headquarters for Detachment D from October 1944 until February 1945.

Madame Fiorella Ferretti Ernst, at left, granddaughter of the Countess of the Chateau La Commanderie, at a neighbor's home, September 1977.

Fulham, London, June 1994 — From left to right, front: Jacques Montpellier, Arnold Franco, and Christiane (née Lorthiois); rear: Tiffaine Bellegarde and Perrine Bellegarde, granddaughter and daughter of Jacques and Christiane.

9th Air Force veterans at the wreath-laying ceremony at the *Arc de Triomphe*, Paris, June 1994.

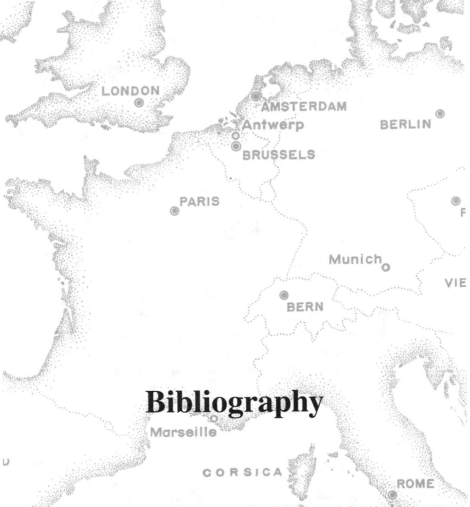

Bibliography

Abner, Alan K. *Dead Reckoning: Experiences of a World War II Fighter Pilot* (Shippensburg, PA: White Mane Publishing, 1997).

Ambrose, Stephen E. *D-Day June 6, 1944: The Climactic Battle of World War II* (New York: Simon & Schuster, 1994).

Ambrose, Stephen E. *Citizen Soldiers: The U.S. Army from the Normandy Beaches to the Bulge to the Surrender of Germany, June 7, 1944-May 7, 1945* (New York: Simon & Schuster, 1997).

Brooks, Thomas R. *The War North of Rome, June 1944-May 1945* (New York: Sarpedon, 1996).

Browning: The Poetical Works of Robert Browning. (Boston, MA: Houghton Mifflin Company, 1974).

Calvocoressi, Peter. *Top Secret Ultra: How the British Intelligence Monitored and Broke the Nazi Top-Secret Code* (New York: Pantheon Books, 1980).

Chevrillon, Claire. *Code Name Christiane Clouet: A Woman in the French Resistance* (College Station: Texas A&M University Press, 1995).

Dunnigan, James F., and Albert A. Nofi. *Dirty Little Secrets of World War II: Military Information No One Told You* (New York: William Morrow, 1994).

Dupuy, Trevor Nevitt. *Hitler's Last Gamble: The Battle of the Bulge, December 1944-January 1945* (New York: Harper Collins, 1994).

Finneran, Richard J., ed. *The Poems of W. B. Yeats: A New Edition* (New York: Macmillan Publishing Co., 1983).

Folkestead, William B. *The View from the Turret* (Shippensburg, PA: White Mane Publishing, 1996).

Franco-Hasson, Elisa. *Il Etait Une Fois L'Ile Des Roses* (Clepsydre Beersel, Belgium).

Gantter, Raymond. *Roll Me Over: An Infantryman's World War II* (New York: Ivy Books, 1997).

Haldane, R. A. *The Hidden War* (New York: St. Martin's Press, 1978).

Hastings, Max. *Overlord: D-Day and the Battle for Normandy* (New York: Simon & Schuster, 1984).

Hinsley, F. H. and Alan Stripp, eds. *Codebreakers: The Inside Story of Bletchley Park* (New York: Oxford University Press, 1994).

Hoobler, Dorothy. *An Album of World War II* (New York: Franklin Watts, 1977).

Howe, George F. *United States Cryptologic History, Series IV, World War II*, Vol. I, *American Signal Intelligence in Northwest Africa and Western Europe (U)* (Washington, D.C.: National Security Agency/Central Security Service, 1980).

Illustrated Story of World War II (Pleasantville, NY: Reader's Digest Association, 1969).

Johnston, John H. *English Poetry from the First World War* (Princeton, NJ: Princeton University Press, 1964).

Jones, R.V. *The Wizard War* (New York: Coward, McCann & Geoghegan, 1978).

Kahn, David. *Seizing the Enigma: The Race to Break the German U-Boat Codes, 1939-1943* (Boston, MA: Houghton Mifflin Co., 1991).

Lee, Bruce. *Marching Orders: The Untold Story of WWII* (New York: Crown Publishers, 1995).

Lewin, Ronald. *Ultra Goes to War: The First Account of World War II's*

Greatest Secret Based on Official Documents (New York: McGraw-Hill Book Co., 1978).

Lewin, Ronald. *The American Magic: Codes, Ciphers & the Defeat of Japan* (New York: Farrar, Straus & Giroux, Inc., 1982).

Life Magazine. *Picture History of World War II* (New York: Time, Inc., 1950).

MacDonald, Callum. *The Lost Battle: Crete 1941* (New York: The Free Press, 1993).

MacDonald, Charles B. *A Time for Trumpets: The Untold Story of the Battle of the Bulge* (New York: William C. Morrow, 1997).

McCue, Paul. *Operation Bulbasket* (London, England: Pen & Sword, 1996).

Meilinger, Phillip S. *Hoyt S. Vandenberg: The Life of a General* (Bloomington: Indiana University Press, 1989).

Orfalea, Gregory. *The Lost Battalion* (New York: The Free Press, 1997).

Petrow, Richard. *The Bitter Years: The Invasion and Occupation of Denmark and Norway, April 1940-May 1945* (New York: William Morrow & Co., 1974).

Putney, Diane. *Allied "Y" Intelligence and the Daylight Air War in Europe* (Washington, D.C.: Office of Air Force History, 1996).

Rudyard Kipling: Selected Verse (New York: Penguin Books, Ltd., 1977).

Shakespeare, William. *King Richard II*, Act II, Scene II.

Stroud, Carsten. *Iron Bravo: Hearts, Minds, and Sergeants in the U.S. Army* (New York: Bantam Books, 1995).

Terkel, Studs. *The Good War: An Oral History of World War Two* (New York: Pantheon Books, 1984).

Thompson, R. W. *D-Day: Spearhead of the Invasion* (New York: Ballantine, 1968).

Toland, John. *The Last 100 Days* (New York: Random House, 1966).

Unit Histories of 3rd RSM (G). (Washington, D.C.: Office of Air Force History).

Whiting, Charles. *The Last Assault — 1944: The Battle of the Bulge Reassessed* (New York: Sarpedon, 1994).

Wilkinson, James D. *Remembering World War II: The Perspective of the Losers* (The American Scholar, 1985).

Wilson, George. *If You Survive* (New York: Ivy Books, 1987).

Index

by Lori L. Daniel